jane packer

flowers

design

philosophy

conran OCTOPUS

jane packer

flowers
design
philosophy

photography by Catherine Gratwicke
styling by Lesley Dilcock

text with Sharon Amos

First published in 2000 by Conran Octopus Limited
a part of Octopus Publishing Group
2–4 Heron Quays
London E14 4JP
www.conran-octopus.co.uk

Reprinted 2001

Commissioning Editor *Stuart Cooper*
Managing Editor *Helen Ridge*
Executive Art Editor *Alison Barclay*
Design *Broadbase*
Production *Alex Wiltshire, Sarah Tucker*

A catalogue record for this book is available from the
British Library

ISBN 1 84091 141 7

Printed in China

contents

At last, it's official. Everyone agrees with what I've believed all along: flowers are hip! People are buying flowers more than ever before, not just as gifts or sympathy tributes, as they did when I first started in the business, but for themselves, and flower arranging is a fashionable occupation.

Where you buy your flowers and how you arrange them says a lot about you; there are definite style do's and don'ts. In some ways this has to be good news, but the flip side of the coin is that designer flowers have brought with them a certain pretentiousness. But I've always felt passionately that people shouldn't feel inhibited about buying or using flowers, and this book shows that there are some very simple rules to follow that make buying and arranging flowers easy. Treat the book like a foundation course, and once you've mastered the basics, which shouldn't take long, you'll have all the skills and confidence you need to go off and do your own thing.

philosophy

elements

Where exactly do you begin when choosing flowers? In a shop, very often the first thing that catches the eye is colour. Once you've picked up a single stem or a bunch, shape and texture come into play as you add more flowers. Other points to bear in mind include the container you plan to use: is it coloured, is it textured, how tall is it? What about the room where the flowers will be displayed? If the flowers are a gift, you will need to consider the character of the person they are intended for – a bouquet can be bold or delicate, romantic or exotic. In this chapter I've covered each separate element of a successful arrangement – colour, shape and texture – and then looked at how to put them together successfully. Of course, in many cases, these elements overlap, but each one has a specific contribution to make. At the same time, you need to bear in mind the height of the flowers and how many stems to use. Finally, scent may, or may not, have a role to play.

colour

We are all becoming more experienced
and adventurous at choosing colours for our homes, as the
ever-expanding market in home-interest magazines and
television programmes proves. Choosing flowers to match
an interior uses exactly the same principles as decorating.

Flower colours go in and out of fashion,
just as colours do in the home and on the
catwalk. Some shades, too, are not obvious
flower colours. For example, green is taken
for granted as the colour of leaves and stems,
yet more and more green flowers are coming
on to the market; while brown, astonishingly,
is one of the newest colours to be developed.

The colour wheel is something you come
across time and time again when colour is
mentioned. It's a circular version of the
rainbow, featuring red, orange, yellow, green,
blue, indigo and violet, arranged anti-
clockwise. In general, colours close together
in the spectrum create a harmonious effect,
while colours opposite each other create a
strong contrast. I tend to prefer toning
colours, which are shades of one base colour
– look at the lilac, pink and purple in the
colour bar on the right – as they are easy on
the eye, but I do use contrasting colours
when I want a much more dramatic effect.

Colour is intensely emotional and can be
used to create or enhance a mood. Fiery
red and orange flowers are ideal for a bold
interior, while blues and purples are better in
a relaxed setting. But when I'm teaching I
like to create recipes for colour that people
feel secure with, rather than give rules to
obey. On the following pages I'll show you
some flower colours and ways of using them.
Once you've mastered a few simple colour
creations, you should feel confident enough
to experiment with your own ideas.

purple & blue

Although this isn't a finished arrangement – the violets are being conditioned by soaking them in water to make them last longer – it illustrates perfectly how closely related colours like purples and blues work together. The colours are muted and soft, and the hint of pink in the blue bowl adds warmth to the whole look. Anemones, tulips, lisianthus and alliums come in similar shades of violet.

green

In the past few years, growers have taken note of interiors and lifestyle trends and developed flowers to suit, like this green chrysanthemum. Green flowers are ideal for schemes with a strong East-meets-West feel; they remind me of Zen gardens where green mosses and foliage predominate. Green is also a soothing and restful colour. Look out for green roses, zinnias and anthuriums, too.

orange

Orange is one of those colours that's been in and out of fashion. When I began working in the 1970s orange 'Enchantment' lilies were all the rage. Downgraded for some years as the unsubtle colour of garage-forecourt flowers, orange is now back at the forefront of flower fashion. These pyracantha berries make a cheerful splash of colour in autumn. Poppies, ranunculus, gerberas, roses and fritillarias are also available in similar full-strength orange.

brown

Brown flowers are another result of changing trends in interior-decorating schemes. Growers have come up with brown flowers, to complement rooms where the emphasis is on neutral colours and natural suedes and leathers. These are not traditional russet tones, though, but true chocolate browns with real shock value – and just as indulgent as a box of chocolates. Look out for banksia, chrysanthemums (pictured), freesias, gerberas and roses.

shape

Flowers and foliage can be classified
under three basic shapes. First there are full, round
flowers that give an arrangement density and form.
Then tall stems of either flowers or foliage add height
and structure. Finally, there are 'filler' plants that do
just that – fill the gaps between the other two shapes.

If you are selecting flowers for a mixed display, these three groups are particularly important. Using different shapes in an arrangement requires you to develop a sense of balance. For example, globular flowers on long stalks at the edge of the design will form a series of ugly heavy blobs. I tend to keep round shapes cut low for a visually balanced look. Typical round flowers include hydrangeas, chrysanthemums, roses and anemones, all of which offer a range of circular shapes, from flat, almost two-dimensional, anemones through to the great globular heads of hydrangeas.

Taller stems work best towards the outside of an arrangement, whether they are bare bamboo and kangaroo tails, which are stark and modern, or delphiniums and gladioli, which give a softer outline.

To fill in the spaces left between solid blooms and linear leaves and stems, you need a hazy plant with an indistinct form, and this is where filler plants with an amorphous shape are invaluable. The classic example is gypsophila – an old favourite – whose blurry clouds of small flowers permeate the arrangement perfectly. Other similarly useful plants include golden rod, September asters and rosemary, which can all be used to fill the spaces between the main components. Although there's nothing to stop you using them on their own, they are not generally the main focus of an arrangement.

There's a definite link between the basic shape of the plant materials you use and the choice of vase. The flowers provide the clue to the container and choosing one is largely a matter of common sense. Tall flowers, for reasons of stability as well as aesthetics, should be matched to a tall vase; put them in a small one and they will topple over the minute you turn your back. Stems of delphiniums and gladioli, for example, also need narrow containers to hold them upright.

The traditional florist's rule states that, for a balanced arrangement, the tallest stems should be no longer than the height of the vase plus half as much again. This is the safe way to arrange flowers, and it truly does work. You really do have to learn, and appreciate, traditional techniques before you start to break the rules. And there is a determined move afoot to break them: tall vases with tiny flowers almost sitting on the neck of the vase, for example, are currently at the cutting edge of designing with flowers.

Texture is an important and exciting part

of any arrangement. When plants or flowers have an amazing texture, it's one instance where choice of colour comes a definite second. Texture has an enormous influence on mood and can be used to suggest very different effects.

Spiky plants such as eryngium and ginger lilies (*Heliconia*) are dynamic and bold, while multi-petalled peonies and roses are voluptuous and feminine. Although I hate to say it, flowers do lend themselves to gender stereotyping. It just wouldn't be right to have blowsy peonies in a male-dominated environment, for example; you'd reserve them for a beauty salon or a bridal salon where their romantic qualities are more likely to be appreciated. An all-male office will generally feel far more comfortable with angular, architectural stems of bird-of-paradise flowers (*Strelitzia*), spiky banksias and unfussy bamboos and grasses.

Texture has a noticeable influence on how we perceive colour: shiny petals reflect more light than soft papery ones and make colours seem brighter and more intense. Delphinium petals, for example, can be almost iridescent, like butterfly wings. Even where the colour doesn't vary with surface texture, a mass of complexly folded and curved petals is far more interesting to look at than a smooth block of solid colour. I love ranunculus flowers: they are packed with petals and are as extravagant and intricate as the showiest

ballgowns with layers and layers of tulle. Petals also add an intensity of colour by creating shadow in their depths.

Some flowers are unbelievably glossy. I didn't really like anthurium flowers when you could only buy them in flamingo pink because, to me, they looked just like plastic. But now green, brown and bruise-purple shades have been developed that complement that high-gloss shine perfectly.

Texture is particularly important when it comes to choosing foliage. Leaves may appear uniformly green, but they are far from it. The surface of a leaf can be glossy, deeply veined or bristling with hairs, all of which affect the overall final impression of colour. Including a range of textures when mixing foliage is vital: if every leaf is shiny, no matter how different the shape, they will all 'melt' into an indistinguishable gloss.

Perhaps the most obvious aspect of texture is touch. I find the stems of pussy willow in spring almost irresistible; the soft furry clumps of flowers remind me of little mouse ears. And I love to stroke the crushed-velvet flowers of celosia. But spiny, thistly eryngiums say, quite firmly, hands off.

spiky **Awesomely armed with spines, eryngium flowers (above) come in different sizes; the smallest are an intense blue, the largest silver grey.** Below, from left **Banksia barely seems a flower – it is more like the mass of wires you'd expect to find inside a telephone exchange. Horse chestnuts have irregular spiny cases, in complete contrast to the shiny fruits within (see opposite, above). The petals of tropical heliconia overlap like reptilian scales and bring a dynamic architectural element to an arrangement.**

shiny Rich glossy conkers (above), gathered in the autumn, shine with the patina of well-polished wood, but fade with time. Below, from left The broad glossy leaves of the aspidistra are now much in demand as cut foliage. Anthurium flowers look as though they have been moulded from plastic rather than grown. The leaves of the familiar garden shrub red robin (*Photinia*) have a high gloss tinged with red and neatly serrated edges, making them popular with florists.

soft **Study the strange soft and furry heart of a protea (above) and you could be looking at a prehistoric flower.** Below, from left Shadows within a red rose are as deep and soft as black velvet. Coxcomb celosia has complexly folded and frilled flowers that are densely furred; cut low and mixed with taller flowers, it looks like a wide band of ribbon wound between the stems. The feathery species of celosia have colourful soft plumes of flowers.

organic Texture doesn't have to be confined to flowers and foliage. Weatherworn slabs of rock (above) can add texture to an arrangement, as can bark from a cork oak (below left), wrinkled as an elephant's hide and colonized with yellow and orange lichens. The sculptural form of a gourd (below centre) resembles an ancient terracotta urn. Fresh green lotus seed heads (below right) will eventually dry to brown. Use their ribbed and pitted forms to punctuate an arrangement with texture.

combining flowers

Putting together different flowers and foliage for an arrangement is like putting food on a plate. You want to achieve something stimulating and exciting. Just as with food, colour is critical. If you were serving macaroni cheese, you wouldn't add mashed potato and cauliflower – the effect would be bland in the extreme. Although each component has good points, they would blur into each other. This is where texture and shape help. Choosing a mixture of spiky and soft textures, and rounded and linear shapes, can define each element of the arrangement. Colours can be combined in many different ways, as you will see. The most elusive ingredient you can add is scent, which follows no rules or boundaries.

Very often that cliché of our times, less is more, is a good maxim to follow when combining flowers. A huge vaseful of flowers is dramatic but I know that one little flower floating in a bowl can have an impact equal to that of the most lavish display.

harmonious colour

The safest way to start experimenting

with colour is to use harmonious colours. By this I mean shades that are simply tones of one base colour. All you need to do is choose your base colour, then add layers of toning colour. For example, you could start with purple and then add violet and lilac. With orange as your starting point, you might add apricot and peach.

How you choose an initial colour depends on the project in hand, but it won't necessarily be the flowers that dictate the colour. For an interior arrangement you might start with the wall colour and then find a toning vase, as pictured here. All sorts of disparate elements can be drawn into the colour scheme, from a table runner or candles to an additional vase. The simple bunch of grape hyacinths at the heart of the arrangement pictured opposite seems to expand as its colour is echoed by the assembled objects.

Flowers for a table setting can be linked to the colour of the napkins, the cloth or even the place-setting cards. I have been known to go for the ultimate in harmonizing colours and match flowers to food, by picking up the shades of summer berries used for the pudding in the petals of roses or peonies, for example. One trick of mine is to reinforce the association by placing the flowers in a glass vase within a larger one, with the gap between filled with berries.

If you are choosing flowers for a bride, the starting point could be the colour of the dress, or even her complexion if you are making a headdress. Just decide on your base colour and expand on it and you can't go wrong. But there's one thing that you shouldn't do. Beware of trying to add white to your arrangement: it can kill that carefully achieved harmony stone dead.

You can also create tonal harmonies with colour, by using shades that are not necessarily close to each other on the colour wheel, but have the same depth of colour. A good way to check whether flowers are similar in tone is to imagine them in black and white – looking through half-closed eyes helps. Colours of the same tone appear as a matching shade of grey.

Harmonious colours are ideal if you want to create an understated, sophisticated effect. The finished arrangement will be quite restrained – it won't leap out or shout at you – but it will be extremely elegant.

contrasting colour

Dramatic arrangements rely on

contrasting colours: strong, powerful shades that compete for attention. Contrasting colours are much harder to use than harmonious shades; their power and intensity need careful handling to create a glorious explosion of colour rather than something that's actually uncomfortable to look at.

For years we've been told that orange and pink just don't 'go' together, or that 'red and green should never be seen', but there are ways of breaking the rules to create successful combinations that don't prompt you to reach for dark glasses. Making use of shape and texture can help you to put strong colours side by side. An interesting outline or a texture that breaks up the surface reduces any negative effect that the undiluted colours might have on each other.

I like to start by looking at nature. Take the spindle berry (*Euonymus europaeus*), which in autumn has shocking-pink fruits that open to reveal bright orange seeds – but it hasn't been banned from gardens or hedgerows because it clashes. Use it as the inspiration behind a pink vase full of bright orange tulips. If you want to increase the shock value still further, set the arrangement against a lime-green wall: it will look brilliant.

Once again, I like to make a comparison between working with flowers and cooking. In my eyes, adding lime to an arrangement – especially one that uses pink – is just like squeezing lime juice over food. It sharpens

the whole effect. As with harmonious colours, you still have to be careful about introducing white, as it will destroy the explosion of colour you've just created. If you still find orange and pink headache-inducing, just move round a slot or two on the colour wheel and pair orange with crimson or purple instead.

Plenty of other colour contrasts occur as a matter of course in nature. Red flowers, such as roses or salvias, held on green stems and with green foliage, are a natural example of complementary colours in action: red and green are exact opposites on the colour wheel. Other complementary pairs include blue and orange, and yellow and violet, all of which create a strong colour contrast without fear of clashing.

For a more restrained colour contrast, consider a pink rose on which green streaks from the stem spread upwards to tinge the base of the petals, and build on that existing contrast. Start with the pink roses and then increase the green in the arrangement by adding stems of the guelder rose, whose rounded flowers are a soft shade of green.

combining
shapes

There is an art to mixing shapes. Every element in an arrangement contributes shape – from the container to the plant material, even the stems below the waterline in a glass vase. I like to break the rules as often as possible in this area, and particularly enjoy creating a contrast between round shapes and graphic lines for the shock value it generates.

In the tall arrangement shown here, I've used the globular blooms of amaryllis to echo the fish-bowl vase filled with apples; the straight flower stems bursting up through the vase are in dramatic contrast. You can make a similar contrast between graphic lines versus soft curves by using a square glass tank to hold a dome of velvety roses. Although the contrast is less marked, you still see the disparity between the heavy square container and the soft flowers. Then, below water, the spiky stems contrast with the crab apples.

Even when you're creating a display based primarily on contrasting shape and form, you can't ignore colour. Linking the colour of the flowers with the other materials used gives an arrangement a sense of harmony. Adding orange satsumas to red roses just because they are round wouldn't have the same effect.

These arrangements gain substance by using just one species of flower. It's a look not restricted to large-headed blooms; you could fill a square tank with a mass of snowdrops, with small white pebbles below the waterline. Whether you choose crab apples, pebbles, gravel, shells, beads or rocks to fill a vase, their role is functional and decorative, holding stems in place as well as lifting up short-stemmed flowers.

Two different arrangements that rely on the contrast between soft curves and straight lines. Water adds another dimension to the displays, magnifying the submerged fruits.

combining texture

The texture of a leaf or a flower helps it to stand out from an arrangement and justify its inclusion. It's all too easy to fall into the trap of combining like with like, without realizing it. For example, marigolds, gerberas and zinnias are all pretty flowers with feathery petals but an arrangement including all three would be boring, especially as their flower heads are very similar shapes.

There's no point in making a selection of foliage if everything you choose has a matt surface, as you won't be able to distinguish between the leaves when they're grouped together. Look for at least two different foliages of opposite textures – shiny versus matt, ribbed versus furry – and look at the texture of the flowers at the same time as you are choosing them for colour. In the arrangement pictured here, there are six very individual ingredients: shiny red robin (*Photinia*) leaves; matt eucalyptus foliage; feathery marigold (*Calendula*) flowers; waxy brown freesias; shiny orange berries and dry papery scabious seed heads.

Part of my trademark style is to group one variety of flowers together within an arrangement rather than intermingle them throughout the display. I've taken the inspiration for this technique directly from nature. After all, in a flowerbed you see a whole clump of foliage or a mass of flowers, not just a single stem sticking up – unless, that is, you happen to be looking at an old-fashioned municipal planting scheme. When combining textures, this technique becomes very important, since it allows a much more dramatic comparison between them, as the finished arrangement illustrates.

A dramatic textural arrangement in browns, orange and ochre (right) is in direct contrast to the simple display of scabious seed heads (far right).

height & number

Whether it's the next trend in ways of arranging flowers, or new material to work with, in floristry there's a constant search for something new. One relatively unexplored way of creating something different is to experiment with height. Although the traditional rule that the tallest stems should be no longer than the height of the vase plus half as much again is well worth learning, there will come a time when you'll feel ready to ignore that maxim and try new things.

By taking one tall glass vase and using it in three different ways, I can show you what I mean. There's a growing trend to submerge flowers in water, but here I've encased a single gerbera within the vase and held it in place with a layer of stones. I like the way the stem twists naturally in the vase, and how the flower looks like a preserved prized specimen.

The green chrysanthemums break the rule, as their tall stems have been cut so that the flowers sit on the rim of the vase. To prevent undue emphasis on the stems – which, let's face it, are not that interesting – I've added a swathe of aspidistra leaf as camouflage.

You'll also come across the rule that flowers should be arranged in odd numbers, a rule devised chiefly to prevent the flowers from looking regimented. But when you're working with something as extraordinary as the kangaroo tails (*Xanthorrhea australis*) on the far left, whose impressive brown spikes become studded with tiny white flowers as they open, you can see there's really no danger of that happening. Similarly, the paired stems of crab apples look sufficiently informal as they are, particularly as some of the fruits have fallen into the water.

Go ahead and break the rules with (from left) stems of kangaroo tails, a single gerbera, a bunch of chrysanthemums, and paired crab apple stems.

scent

Fragrance is an incredible part of my job. Even though my nose has been bombarded with so many different scents over the years, it never fails to respond to certain situations, such as the first narcissi of the year being prepared in the shop.

Left, from top **Highly perfumed 'Casablanca' lilies have a strong exotic scent that can quickly fill a small space; hothouse stephanotis flowers are sweetly scented, as are those of spring-flowering lily of the valley; the classic freesia offers a neat and unobtrusive way to add scent to an arrangement, and is available all year round.** Opposite **An image of intense decadence and seduction as rose petals crushed underfoot release their intoxicating scent.**

Every spring the unmistakable fragrance of narcissi transports me back to when I was given my very first pay packet and dithered over whether to buy the new Diana Ross single or a big bunch of 'Soleil d'Or'. Not surprisingly, I chose the flowers.

Scent evokes memory and emotion in all of us, and it can come from the most unprepossessing of plants. Walking across the park one grey day, I was hit by a sudden burst of fragrance from a spiky mahonia bush; its yellow flowers smelled as sweet as lily of the valley. Eleagnus, which we tend to use as a foliage plant, is another surprisingly fragrant species, producing the most insignificant but wonderfully perfumed flowers in winter.

Scent is seasonal. At Christmas the shop is filled with the rich perfume of cloves, pine and cinnamon. Yet the moment Christmas is over and we step into spring, scented narcissi and hyacinths predominate, while summer is characterized by the heady perfume of roses, lilac and honeysuckle.

You must be careful how you use scented flowers. They can be inappropriate at a dinner table, competing with the food; and the heady perfume of lilies or gardenias in a small sitting room can be stifling. Gifts for friends who are ill or in hospital can include scented species; lavender is innately calming, as is the foliage of scented geraniums, but avoid anything more overpowering. Foliage is a good way of adding scent to an arrangement: think of aromatic rosemary, clean-smelling eucalyptus and pine-scented evergreens.

materials & techniques

To choose all the ingredients for an arrangement – whether it's a simple posy or a bridal bouquet – you need to follow a train of thought. This can be triggered by the colour of the flowers, the mood you're aiming to create, even the architecture of the room where the flowers will be displayed. The simplest idea can be a useful starting point. When I discuss flowers for a special occasion with a customer, very often I gain a clue to what to use just from meeting them and getting a hint of their personality. There may, of course, be a specific theme that the flowers can contribute to – a 21st birthday or a wedding anniversary, for example. As well as selecting flowers and foliage, you may need to choose fabric, paper, ribbons or tulle, plus beads and wire, to complete the arrangement. Specialist accessory shops and the haberdashery departments of large stores are good sources of ribbons, cord, lace and other trimmings – but don't leave it at that. Experiment!

pot plants

There was a universal trend in the 1970s to fill the home with pot plants: spider plants cascaded over bookshelves, while cheese plants sprouted from dried-out, moss-covered poles and straggled round the room. This fashion for foliage spread to the office, where large ugly shiny-leaved plants were displayed in white tubs that fast gathered cigarette butts and crumpled plastic coffee cups. I should know: it was then my job to clear out the tubs and polish the leaves.

Thank goodness cut flowers replaced the foliage plants, as they became more affordable and available. But what goes around comes around, and now pot plants are back in the limelight again. Orchids have played a major role in reviving house plants in the style stakes. Like any new fashion, they began as exclusive items, but then gradually worked their way down the scale, so that now you can buy an orchid to take home along with the weekly supermarket shop.

It all started with the white moth orchid (*Phalaenopsis*), which looks expensive and exotic. Now growers have developed coloured varieties that can be accessorized with matching or contrasting containers and gravels. To customize a plant so that it harmonizes with an interior, try standing it inside a coordinating container rather than attempting to repot it. Flowering plants need their roots restricted so that they put all their energy into blooming. If you give the roots more space, flowering may be reduced. Leaving a plant in its original pot also makes it easier to water; you can lift it out and water it without damaging the container.

A berried branch takes the place of a plain supporting bamboo cane, and raffia ties have been used instead of wire twists, to add extra interest to a purple phalaenopsis orchid (left). A contrasting turquoise pot suits a yellow dendrobium orchid; the final flourish is a topping of shocking-pink gravel.

Today people want more than just a plant

in a pot. A plant needs to work hard to justify its inclusion in an interior-decorating scheme; it has to be a stylish accessory that enhances a room. Pot plants are no longer primarily seen as living things. Instead they've become integral – but ultimately disposable – design accessories.

Opposite **This is the way to make house plants look modern again – even that staid old fogey, the Christmas cactus. In this group, white flowers and white variegated foliage have been linked by white glass and ceramic containers. The plants are (from left) a white-flowered Christmas cactus, two succulents, an aloe vera, a grass (*Scirpus*) and mind-your-own-business (*Soleirolia soleirolii*).**

Left **To create a contemporary display of traditional spring bulbs for an ultra-modern setting, I stood individual pots in a huge glass tank packed with lichen moss, to conceal them. A decorative band of twisted larch twigs breaks up the strong lines of the tank.**

containers

There was a time when vases were kept in a cupboard and only brought out when they were needed. Now they are very much a part of our everyday décor, even when empty. I have an inexhaustible appetite for containers. I love grouping them for display, and when I'm not filling them with flowers I arrange them by texture or colour, as I would flowers.

Fashions in containers and vases come and go. Once upon a time absolutely every arrangement from florists was presented in a basket of some sort; current trends include lines of identical vases or arrangements in containers of staggered heights. Every home-interest shop and department store has shelves of vases to choose from, but containers don't have to be exclusive. Simple milk bottles or jam jars can be just as much fun as an expensive designer piece – and perhaps show more imagination.

You can use containers to shape the direction an arrangement takes and to change the image of a flower completely. A single delphinium stem in a tall streamlined glass vase is a million miles away from its traditional cottage-garden image, while an exotic glory lily is brought down to earth when stood in a gaudy recycled tin can.

Right **Toning ceramic vases in a variety of rounded and squared-off shapes make a pleasing display with or without flowers.** Opposite **A white-skinned amaryllis bulb in a funnel-shaped ceramic container makes a strong statement. As the amaryllis grows, the container will make a good visual counterbalance to the strong spear-like bud.**

Four eclectic groups of containers show how displaying by colour and texture works. Decide on a colour first, then keep an eye out for pieces wherever you go: junk shops and artists' exhibitions, for example. Include every shape and size imaginable and every material, too, from pottery to steel, glass to stone.

different container, different effect

The most commonly made mistake in flower arranging is to choose the wrong container. Here I've used parrot tulips to demonstrate what a difference the shape of a container can make to how flowers look and behave.

The wide-mouthed vase in the top left corner has straight sides that hold the flowers neatly upright, so there's not a lot that can go wrong. To exaggerate the vertical still further, I've added slightly taller straight stems of pussy willow to draw the eye upwards.

In complete contrast, the flared-neck vase (beneath) is one of the hardest to get right. With an extra-wide neck you need far more flowers than you may realize at first, or you're left with a gaping hole in the centre. Each of these two vases contains a similar number of flowers, yet the display in the wide-necked vase looks open, loose and relaxed, while there appear to be far more blooms in the straight-sided vase. To get the best effect when arranging flowers in a flared-neck vase, work round the edge first, then slot more stems into the centre to fill the space.

The short square tank arrangement is an ideal way of extending the life of tulips. They carry on growing after they've been cut but, as they do so, their stems become weaker, giving them that droopy look. By cutting them down to size to fit the tank once they've reached that stage, you cut away the droopiness and get a whole new effect.

The narrower and taller the vase, the fewer flowers you need. The slim vase has just four tulips, each one tied to a pussy willow twig with a piece of raffia to hold it upright and avoid a spreadeagled effect as the flowers age.

Clockwise from top left

The straight sides of a vase hold the tulips upright. Cutting tulips low in a square tank gives them no opportunity to droop. Pussy willow twigs and raffia keep tulip stems straight in a narrow vase. A flared neck creates a gentle, relaxed effect.

starting with the container

Sometimes you come across a vase or container so stunning that, no matter what flowers or foliage you place in them, they are always going to be secondary to the vase itself. When you are using a real statement piece, the flowers have to work with it: they mustn't hide any aspect of it and should enhance its unique features.

I adore the dramatic cutaway ceramic containers shown here. The holes in the vases demand to be used rather than ignored, and these large variegated leaves are the perfect choice. Even their stems are beautifully splashed with white, echoing the colour of the containers. An alternative with the assurance and poise to carry off a similar effect would be a single arum lily. Its stem would also be flexible enough to bend and twist through the vase without splitting.

In this display the colour and drama of both leaf and container are equally matched, but it might be the colour of the vase, its shape or its extraordinary height that sends you off in search of the right partner.

When using a precious artefact to display flowers or foliage, don't be tempted to fill it with water. Water is notorious for staining, for leaving salt deposits and for lifting glazes or decoration. Instead insert stems in individual florist's water-phials to keep them fresh, and top them up daily; or use a small inner plastic container of water that can't be seen when the flowers are in place.

accessories

With the right accessories you can
emphasize the character of a bloom or give it a
completely new one. An appropriate ribbon or trim is
just as important as the flowers themselves and can make
– or break – your arrangement. Use accessories for
flowers in the same way as you would for yourself: to
dress up or play down whatever you are wearing.

Just as a shawl can soften the outline of a
severely cut dress, so gauzy chiffon ribbon
can emphasize the romantic in a flower
arrangement. Ribbon, cord and braid can be
used to bind flowers or trim a container or
basket, and so create a mood. But be sure
to match your materials to the flowers: for
example, I wouldn't put a wisp of voile with
a big butch banksia – a thick bold cord
would suit it far better. There are plenty of
rustic ribbons, too, such as the woven hessian
shown on the right, and plaited jute. For
voluptuous bows and flounces, look out for
ribbon with wired edges, which can help
you to achieve an effect more easily.

Pebbles finish off a planted arrangement
by disguising the soil, and they can be just
as versatile as braid or ribbon. A handful of
tortoiseshell gravel scattered on the surface
of a pot adds instant rural charm, while
pebbles of polished jet in a clear glass vase
with one or two blooms suggest
contemporary oriental. Other pebble-style
accessories include coloured gravels, which
are generally sold for using in fish tanks, and
bags of tiny shells. Tie in coloured gravels
with the hue of the flowers.

Twine can be an undercover accessory, at
its most basic used for binding stems in a tied
bouquet. I love rough string for its texture.
Sometimes I leave it on show for rustic
simplicity, but I also like to use shocking-pink
or lime-green knitting yarn – whatever tones,
or contrasts, with the flowers. It's all to do
with making your displays stand out from the
crowd and look that little bit different.

Finally, when wrapping flowers think
about the impression you want to give.
Inspiration can come from the most unlikely
sources: pasta packaged in wax paper from
the Italian deli, a parcel of nails from an
old-fashioned hardware store tied up with
string. There really are no barriers to what
can and can't be used. Although, to my
dismay, brown paper has lost its naïve charm
through overuse and overfamiliarity, the chic
yet modest alternative is kraft paper, a strong
paper in sludgy colours available from artists'
suppliers. Use it to play down a bouquet,
to present it as a simple gesture, pared down
to its basic ingredients. But for those times
when you want to appear extravagant,
nothing can beat swathing flowers in layer
upon layer of tissue paper.

Buying a sugar thermometer, digital

scales and a set of copper-bottomed saucepans won't
necessarily make you a better cook – you'll merely be
a better equipped one – and the same goes for flower
arranging. There are a few basic pieces of equipment that
it would be difficult to manage without but, apart from
that, improvization is easy, and it's all down to you.

The one thing you can't do without is a
good pair of florist's scissors. They are worth
investing in; without them you'll end up
blunting every pair of scissors in the house.
Florist's foam makes life easier, too. It's vital
for arrangements that need to last for any
length of time, and for garlands of moss and
flowers that would wilt and die without a
source of moisture. There are several brands
but Oasis is the best known. It comes in
blocks of all shapes and sizes and in two
different types, for wet or dry arrangements.
The version illustrated here is for dry work;
it doesn't absorb water and is stiff and brittle.

Florist's foam for fresh flowers needs
soaking in water before use. I always float it
on top of a bucket of water for a few
minutes before cutting and shaping. There's
no need to force it under the surface. In fact,
if you do, you can end up with an airlock, so
that when you cut the foam to size, the
centre is still completely dry. You can reuse
foam, but it does have a limited life span. For
arrangements that don't use a container there
is designer florist's foam, a layer of foam with
a waterproof backing that protects surfaces
(see also page 85).

Before florist's foam was developed,
arrangements relied on chicken wire to hold
flowers in place. Some traditionalists still
prefer it, but I find it restricts how I work.
Chicken wire holds all the flowers upright,
but with foam you have a choice; you can let
flowers trail by pushing them up through the
foam from below. It's quite easy to cut
chicken wire with scissors, so it doesn't
demand any extra equipment.

If you plan to make wedding bouquets,
headdresses or wreaths, you'll need florist's
wires. These come in a variety of thicknesses
or gauges, and are sold in ready-cut lengths
or on reels. Wait to see what you need for
a specific project rather than buying a
selection as a matter of course. I'd also advise
you to err on the side of caution and buy
the finest-gauge wires. Nothing looks worse
than a stiff, artificial creation. Wires should
be used for gentle support and to lend
flexibility to a flower that's going to be out
of water all day.

Other useful equipment includes things
that you are likely to have at home anyway,
such as plain string and plastic bowls of
varying sizes to fit inside display containers.

techniques

Once you've learnt the basic techniques, you can twist or adapt them to add your own style. But before you can do that it's important to know how a technique works, and why you need to do it in the first place. There are so many techniques to learn, depending on the types of arrangements you intend to create, but the basics I'm going to look at include methods for making sure flowers are in peak condition; cutting flowers; preserving flowers and foliage; and finally, and probably the trickiest, wiring. When you are trying a technique for the first time – particularly wiring – practise first on garden flowers and foliage rather than splashing out on expensive ingredients.

Once you've absorbed the reasons for these techniques, and mastered the methods, you'll have a good grounding that will give you the confidence to experiment and reinvent, so that when fashions in flowers change – as they do very quickly – you can adapt and change, too.

cutting

As soon as cut flowers are out of water, their stems start to dry out. So the top priority as soon as you get them home is to put them in water. But there's no point in doing this unless you re-cut their stems first. Use your florist's scissors for this job. Once the fibres in the stems have started to dry out, it's much harder for them to take up water. But if you cut at least 2cm (just under an inch) from each stem, you expose fresh fibres that will soak up water more easily. Making the cut at an angle increases the surface area exposed to the water, which maximizes uptake. Taking the trouble to re-cut the stems pays dividends: it means that your flowers will last longer and the buds are more likely to open fully.

At the same time as re-cutting the stems, I always strip off the lower leaves from each stem; anything that is going to remain underwater will start to decay quickly, turning the water slimy and smelly. Stocks are notorious for doing this. Once the water turns murky, bacteria flourish and rapidly kill off the flowers.

If I'm using florist's foam, I cut the stems at an even more exaggerated angle, so that they are almost as sharp as a needle. They must be pushed in at least 5cm (2in) to have any chance of taking up water from the foam. In a big display using tall flowers, push the stems in deeper still, to anchor them.

Having spent years standing out in the rain in the backyard hitting woody stems with a mallet in an effort to increase their ability to take up water, I've now learnt that this probably does more harm than good. Rather than opening up the stem to increase the water uptake, it actually smashes the cells so that they can't take up water at all. Instead follow the same rule for soft-stemmed flowers, and cut woody stems at an angle. If the stems are exceptionally hard, make a vertical cut up the stem as well.

Left **Tulips for a tied bouquet need all their stems cut level so that they stand upright in a vase. A few flowers such as daffodils and narcissi actually resent being cut – it makes their stems 'bleed' with a sticky sap. Instead these flowers are pulled from the bulb when harvested. If you have to cut them, a specific flower food will minimize 'bleeding'.** Opposite **A lily of the valley stem cut at an oblique angle to increase water uptake and prolong the life of the flower.**

caring for flowers

Here are some tips for making the most of cut flowers, whether you've bought them yourself or received them as a gift. Some take just a few minutes, others a little longer, but they're all well worth doing.

reviving floppy flowers

Have you ever bought a bunch of flowers and discovered that they were distinctly floppy when you unwrapped them? Well, there is a tried-and-tested technique for reviving them. At the market, flowers may have been out of water for as long as 24 hours after picking, so they do need to be reconditioned. Roses are the most susceptible; they really suffer when they're kept out of water. Follow this emergency revival procedure.

Unwrap the flowers and trim away the lower leaves. This is also the ideal time to pare away rose thorns with an ordinary pocket knife, to make them easier to handle when arranging. Then re-cut the stems as described on page 62. Now wrap the flowers in paper – several sheets of newspaper are ideal. It's vital to use paper rather than plastic, as paper is strong enough to support the flowers yet doesn't make them 'sweat'. Stand the wrapped flowers in a bucket of reasonably deep water. If you're in a hurry, the stems should be recharged with water and strong enough in an hour, but, to be sure, I'd recommend leaving them overnight. On the rare occasions when this method doesn't work, take the flowers back to your florist; they will want to know about it and put it right.

reviving flowers with floppy stems

Flowers such as gerberas may need reviving after being out of water, but the technique is not quite so simple. If you wrap gerberas in newspaper and stand them in water, they will stiffen but may not straighten, and you'll end up with awkward, twisted stems. In the shop we lift them out of the box but leave the packaging around the flower heads intact. We then suspend the flowers from the packaging so that the stems are in a bucket of water but are not supporting the weight of the flowers. The result: strong straight-stemmed gerberas.

Another technique to condition flowers that have been out of water for 24 hours or more is to submerge them in water. This is especially useful for small flowers (see the violets on page 14) and for species such as hellebores that you might cut from your own garden, and which have a tendency to droop.

keeping the water clean

To make flowers last as long as possible you need to change the water daily. This sounds like a bore but it isn't; there's no need to rearrange the flowers every time. All I do is stand the vase in the sink under the cold tap and let the running water do the work. Then lift the vase out and wipe it dry. Always start with a clean vase; dirty vases harbour bacteria that start to decay the flowers. Clean the vase with bleach if necessary and rinse thoroughly afterwards. When I was a junior I was ticked off for not cleaning a vase, and told to imagine it was the equivalent of drinking orange juice out of the same glass every day for a month without washing it up.

Most flowers are sold with a sachet of flower food, containing ingredients to reduce bacteria levels in the water, plus replacement sugars to feed the flowers and encourage any buds to open. It's not just a gimmick, so do use it. I've conducted trials to see how flower food compares with plain water and traditional additives, such as lemonade, and it really does do a good job.

Stains from lily pollen are virtually impossible to remove from clothes and furnishing fabrics, so act as soon as the flowers open. Pull off the stamens while they are still hard and smooth, and before they produce the dusty pollen. Always pull the stamens off with your fingers rather than cutting them off: I can't bear the amputated look that scissors give. If you do get lily pollen on your clothes, never rub or brush it. Use a loop of sticky tape to lift it off.

preserving

Of all the commercial methods of preserving flowers and foliage, freeze-drying is the latest trend. By freezing all the moisture and then blasting it away, it is possible to dry even fleshy fruits like strawberries and all sorts of vegetables for use in arrangements. They have to be varnished though, as they have a tendency to reabsorb moisture from the atmosphere and start to rot.

But at home traditional methods are best. Flowers need to be hung upside down to dry, to produce straight stems and to stop heads from flopping. They also need to be hung in a warm room so that they dry quickly; the longer the process takes, the more likelihood there is of the material rotting. Avoid hanging them in a sunny room, too, as sunlight shrivels them before they have a chance to dry — a greenhouse would be a disaster.

For best results, choose flowers with care. Woody-stemmed species work best. Fleshy-stemmed flowers are much more difficult because they contain so much more water. I'd never try to dry hyacinths for that reason. Although it may be possible to do so, I don't think the end result would look much like a hyacinth — or like anything else you'd particularly want in your home.

Dried leaves make evocative displays in autumn. Placed in a textured bowl, they are an inexpensive and interesting alternative to flowers. Bound together with ribbon, they are poignantly romantic, like a parcel of faded love letters discovered in an attic.

Some things will dry themselves without assistance. Eucalyptus and beech leaves, hydrangeas and proteas all dry beautifully without any help. Foliage can be preserved by standing it in a mixture of glycerine and water. Although I buy stems preserved in this way, I've never actually tried it myself. Most chemists sell glycerine, and an old recipe I came across recommends mixing one part glycerine with two parts water.

Autumn is the time of year when we think about preserving flowers and foliage, in an attempt to hang on to that last burst of colour before it disappears altogether.

wiring

Wiring was invented to extend the life of flowers used out of water, to hold them in place so that they don't droop or wilt. It's an invaluable technique for making headdresses and bridal bouquets. I firmly believe that even though flowers may be wired, they shouldn't look as if they are.

Wiring should be as natural as possible and it should be discreet. It should be strong enough to support flowers but light enough to retain a degree of movement. I can't think of anything worse than a trailing bridal bouquet that is wired ramrod stiff and carried like a tortured shield of wires and flowers. Wiring has a definite purpose but it should be subtle and not take over the arrangement.

Choose a wire to suit the weight of the materials. A tiny leaf needs a fine wire at the back to support it, while a rosebud or lily will need a heavier wire. Bulky items such as apples and pine cones need the toughest gauge of all, to attach them to a wreath. Flowers wired for a bouquet or headdress should be taped to cover any scratchy ends; for wreaths this is not an issue.

Wiring is a daunting technique to master, so it's best to build up speed and confidence by practising on an inexpensive ingredient such as ivy leaves before tackling a bouquet or headdress. Wire up leaf after leaf until you feel you have mastered the technique; it will be time well spent.

Leaves

To wire a leaf, turn it face down and make a small stitch through the top third of the leaf across the vein. Pull the wire through so that one 'leg' is about two-thirds longer than the other. Hold the stitch and fold down the two wires, pinching them on to the leaf stem. Take hold of the end of the longer wire and twist it round the remaining wire and stem (1). The front of the leaf with just a tiny stitch visible (2). The wire makes the leaf flexible (3).

Flowers

The lily of the valley stem shown below has been bound with the lightest and finest wire, a gauge that is as fine as a single hair. The wire has been twisted between each flower so that it supports them gently and stops the stem wilting. This enables you to shape the stem as well. Each end of the wire has been neatened by binding it round the stem. At this point you can add a longer support wire to the base of the stem, if necessary, to give you more length to work with.

The lily shown opposite with its face down (1) needs two wires: a support wire and fine wire. The support wire is pushed down into the stem, while the fine wire is inserted through the base of the flower to hold the petals in place. The fine wire is twisted on to the support wire, and both wires are then covered with florist's tape.

Freesias (2) are classic bridal-bouquet flowers. Here a strand of fine wire has been wound through the buds to stop them drooping, while a separate strand of fine wire has been used to pierce the base of the main flower to hold the petals in place. The ends of the wire are brought down to the stem: if the flower is for a bouquet, a supporting wire can be added now; if it is for a headdress, the wires simply need twisting and taping.

A fine wire has been used to pierce the base of a stephanotis flower (4). One end is then bound round the other and the flower stem to support it.

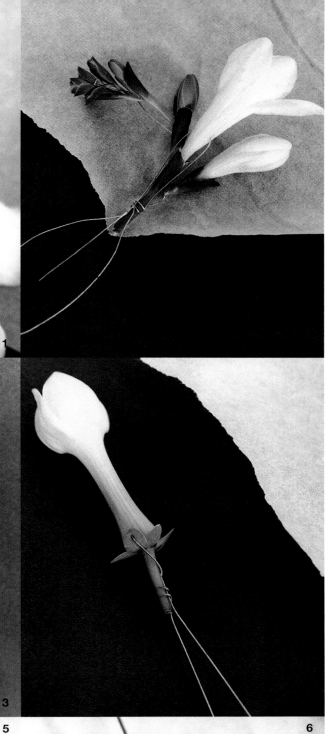

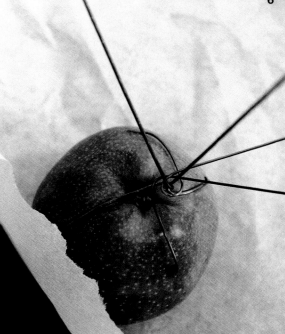

Other items

When wiring fir cones (3), match the wire to the weight. Here a strong steel wire has been bound through the cone's lower scales, then the two ends have been brought down and twisted together a few times before opening them out again. To attach the cone to a wreath, push each wire into the moss through to the other side, bend the wires back, and then push them back through the moss.

When wiring a bundle of decorative dogwood twigs (5), disguise the wire loop that holds them together with raffia or ribbon before wiring the bundle to the wreath. Attach it as you would the fir cone.

An apple (6) is one of the heaviest wreath ingredients you are likely to use. Use two lengths of strong wire and push them through at right angles to each other. Bring the ends below the apple and twist them together before splaying them out to spread the weight when it is attached to the wreath.

designing with flowers

You tend to find that particular colours become associated with certain celebrations: red flowers for a ruby wedding anniversary, white for a wedding or christening, and pumpkin orange for Halloween, and so on. By making maximum use of a single colour, you create a coordinated look that you can keep adding to, to reinforce the theme.

If the occasion is important, everything – flowers, food, décor – needs to look special. To make sure I don't forget anything, I make a list. For example, when I was planning the flowers for a Chinese New Year party, I decided on a theme and then listed all the ways I could add to it. Rather than opting for classic oriental red and white, I began with the papery orange seed heads of Chinese lanterns. I mixed them with actual paper lanterns in orange for a touch of wit, and made a note to order orange napkins and chopsticks tied with orange string, and to use oranges with names written on them as place settings.

party bauble

This is a really versatile decoration. A bauble can make a fun party decoration to hang over a table, at a doorway, even on a Christmas tree, or it can be a beautiful bridesmaid's pomander. Here I've made two baubles using green chrysanthemums and purple carnations for dramatic contrast. They rely on sheer density of colour for their attraction, but you could introduce some foliage for a more rustic look. Pay special attention to choosing cord or ribbon to hang the bauble; you could even add a tassel if appropriate.

1 Take a ready-made sphere of florist's foam or carve your own from a block of foam. Leave it to soak for an hour, then let it drain for at least two hours so that the finished bauble doesn't drip.

2 Cut a length of medium-gauge wire (71 gauge is ideal), long enough to push through the centre of the sphere and to wrap round it. Join the wire to the cord or ribbon by twisting them round each other several times. Push the wire right through the centre of the sphere, so that the join between the wire and cord is hidden inside the sphere. Then shape the wire back against the foam and push the end back down into the top of the foam to secure the wire. If you are making an extra-large bauble, it is a good idea at this point to cover the foam with a layer of chicken wire, to stop it crumbling later on.

3 Cut the flower heads from the main stem, making sure that you leave each flower with a short stem, about 5cm (2in) long. Make the first row of flowers around the equator of the sphere, pushing the stems firmly into the foam.

4 Add a second row of flowers at right angles to the first, before filling in the individual segments. This way the sphere of flowers will retain its shape perfectly. As the flowers are held in moist florist's foam, you can safely make up a bridesmaid's pomander the day before the wedding.

materials

ready-made sphere of florist's
 foam, 13cm (5in) in
 diameter, or a block from
 which to carve your own
length of medium-gauge
 (71 gauge) wire
decorative cord or ribbon
 (the final length will depend
 on how you intend
 displaying the bauble)
20–25 stems of spray
 chrysanthemums or 40
 carnations

alternative flowers
full open species such as
roses, marigolds, ranunculus

moroccan feast

Rose petals strung into garlands like antique tassels make opulent decorations for a special North African evening. They're so quick and easy to prepare – no special techniques or equipment required.

I quite often cook to a theme, and whenever I do I experiment with the flowers for the room decoration, so that I end up with something that links with the food, rather than is at odds with it. One image I can't get out of my mind from my travels in Morocco is that of rose petals. I've stayed in places where rose petals were sprinkled on the pillows at night, and, for me, their colour and fragrance are inextricably linked with the country. So for a Moroccan feast I decided to make garlands of red and pink rose petals, to blend with the earthy terracotta walls and the richly coloured cushions.

Using rose petals is not as extravagant as it appears. For this kind of celebration they need last only for the evening, so top-quality roses aren't necessary. In fact, flowers almost on their last legs will do; all you need is the petals. Twist the flower heads to release the petals, then thread them on to varying lengths of red craft wire. Push the wire right through the centre of the petals, and every so often knot or twist the wire, or thread a bead on, to stagger the pattern and make it more interesting. Knot the wire at the end to stop the petals falling off.

A traditional oval

centrepiece of flowers would be completely at odds with this North African-influenced table. Instead of trying to adapt an inappropriate Western style and force it to suit the occasion, think laterally. Here I've used bowls and glasses from a typical Moroccan place setting to create a display of flowers.

Left **Rose petal 'kebabs'** are made by threading pink and red petals on wire and securing each end with a gold bead.
Above **Rose petals** scattered on the table and tray continue the colour theme.
Opposite **Jewel-coloured tea glasses and tiny bowls**, traditionally used for serving hot harrissa-type sauces, are filled with fuchsia-pink dendrobium orchids and pale pink cymbidium orchids.

totem pole

The classical pedestal arrangement — that stalwart of formal dinners and weddings — has long needed updating. As soon as I see one, it immediately says hotel foyer or church to me. At last I feel I've come up with a modern alternative — a totem pole of flowers — that can be used for all sorts of celebrations.

You will need to find a suitable base. I've used a rough-hewn piece of timber as an unfussy alternative to the typical wrought-iron stand or panelled wooden version.

1 **Carve the foam into the shape you want; here I've cut a tall cylinder. To soak the foam in water, I stood it in the bath for a few hours. Be warned: a soaked block this size is seriously heavy, so, as an alternative, you could build the block from smaller blocks of foam. Stand the foam in a large plant pot saucer to catch the water. Wrap the foam in chicken wire for extra support. If you have used small blocks of foam, the chicken wire will also hold the individual pieces together in place.**

2 **Bring the edges of the chicken wire together and fasten them with lengths of florist's wire. Insert a short length of wire through a hole in each edge, pull it tight and twist round a couple of times, before pushing the cut ends neatly back into the foam. Repeat along the length of the chicken wire.**

3 **Cut the flower stems to about 8–10cm (3–4in), then start to insert them in the foam. You can begin anywhere you like, as there is no focal point to the design, but aim to create small groups of the same flowers, rather than scattering them at random, to give a coherent effect.**

Without foliage the flower heads blend together to create an unbroken mass of colour and texture. To make it even more interesting, I would insert burning incense sticks between the flowers at intervals. Water the top of the totem pole daily to keep it looking good for a week or more.

materials

huge block of florist's foam
large plant pot saucer
roll of chicken wire
heavy-gauge (71 or 90 gauge) florist's wire for joining the edges of the chicken wire
white roses
white carnations
white gerberas
(the exact numbers of flowers will depend on the size of the totem, but you will need masses and masses)
suitable base for the totem

alternative flowers

larger-headed blooms such as sunflowers, peonies, large chrysanthemums, poinsettia heads at Christmas

love heart

The rose has been a symbol of love for centuries, and it is still the quintessential romantic flower. Massed together into a heart shape, the message that roses convey to the recipient is unmistakable.

To make an arrangement like the one pictured here, you will need between 50 and 60 roses. Check that the flowers are in peak condition and that there's not a bruised petal in sight – you don't want to imply anything negative about your feelings! To ensure a long-lasting effect, choose roses that have barely unfurled.

The base of the heart is designer florist's foam. This is made up of a thick sheet of waterproof fibre, topped with a layer of absorbent florist's foam; the benefit of the waterproof layer is that the arrangement can be laid on any surface, even polished wood, without risk of damage.

To make sure I get the heart shape right, I practise first on a sheet of paper, then, when I'm happy with the shape, I use it as a paper template for cutting out the foam.

Before pushing the roses into the foam, it needs to be moistened. Float it, absorbent layer down, in a sink full of water, but don't try to force it under the surface or, as with ordinary florist's foam, you may end up with an airlock. Then cut the roses to length, leaving them with a stem of around 5cm (2in). To create a rounded dome of flowers, cut some stems a little longer and place these in the centre of the design. As you work outwards, trim the stems of the roses to bring the shape down gradually towards the edges of the foam.

Although our rose bushes are bare in February, cut roses are flown in from all over the globe, from growers in countries as far apart as Colombia and Israel, to cater for the huge Valentine's Day demand. Red roses are still traditional Valentine's favourites, but I rather like the subtle tones of the two shades of pink shown in the heart featured here – and they're just as romantic.

Other flowers that can be used to make a love heart include peonies, chrysanthemums, carnations, camellias and – no expense spared – gardenias. As with roses, leave some of the stems a little longer to make a softly rounded dome. Alternatively, you could cover the heart with deep green velvety bun moss, embellished with just three or four flowers.

This exquisite heart is packed with roses
in shades of pink, each one as perfect and unblemished as an icing-sugar rose. Don't just make one for Valentine's Day; use it as a centrepiece for a wedding table, as an engagement gift, or present one to your mum on Mother's Day.

love token

Can you imagine anything more decadent than discovering your bathroom strewn with roses? Here I've indulged my wildest fantasies and created a bath mat made entirely from rose petals. It looks far too beautiful to step on, yet crush the heart you must, to reach a romantic bathtub of roses.

You'll need 20–30 yellow roses and ten pink ones to make the mat, plus extra flowers to scatter on the bath water. Although this is an extravagant gesture, you don't need top-quality roses; buy the cheapest you can, as they don't need to look perfect or last long.

Before dismissing the rose petal mat as a completely over-the-top idea, think of ways to use it to mark other occasions. Reduced in size, the design would make beautiful place settings at a special dinner, for example. To make the heart-shaped pattern, cut a paper template and lay it on the floor in front of the bath. Strip the

petals from the roses by twisting each head from the stem. Scatter the yellow petals around the heart shape. When they are in place, lift up the paper and fill the space left with pink petals. Finally, run a bath and float some roses on the water. Strip off any thorns before you do this, or passions may run high for the wrong reasons.

materials

about 3 stephanotis plants, to
  give just over 100 florets
fine silver florist's wires
  (36 gauge)
supporting florist's wires
  (56 gauge)
florist's tape
1.5m (1½yd) of ribbon

alternative flowers
gardenia flowers and leaves,
tuberose flowers, white
agapanthus bells with ivy,
camellia or small laurel leaves

This wired posy, about 20cm (8in) across, is elegant in its simplicity and sweetly scented. I can picture it being carried by a bride wearing a simple satin gown, perhaps 1950s style, with sleek hair and strong make-up.

1 Separate the flowers into florets. Pierce the base of each one, as though making a small stitch, with the fine silver wire. Pull the wire through and, holding a supporting wire against the stem, secure everything in place by winding one end of the silver wire tightly round the other end of the wire, the stem and the supporting wire.

2 Wrap florist's tape around each flower stem to hold the supporting wire firmly in place.

3 The domed shape of the posy is made by taping the stems together at the binding point – about 10cm (4in) below the tip of the florets. Make a fan

shape, taping the stems together as you go. Make another fan crossing the first at right angles. Fill in the four sections with individual stems.

4 Bind all the stems together with florist's tape.

5 Wire the leaves by making a small stitch with a silver wire through the top third of each leaf, across the central vein. Hold a supporting wire against the stem and proceed as in step 1.

Position the leaf stems evenly around the outside of the posy, taping in each one at the binding point. Trim all the stems and tape them together to make a smooth handle. To cover the handle with ribbon, leave about 50cm (20in) of ribbon hanging free and, beginning at the top, twist it tightly round the handle, overlapping it neatly. When you reach the bottom, wind the ribbon back up the handle in the same way. Tie the two ends in a bow.

bridal bouquets

Fashions in bridal flowers wax and wane as quickly as the styles of wedding dresses. When I first began to design wedding flowers for the fashion pages of magazines and newspapers, voluminous ballgown skirts were all the rage, and the look was dreamy and romantic. Flowers followed suit, with huge bouquets of wild tumbling foliage and petals mirroring the vast skirts. Combined with heavy full circlets for headdresses, the effect was almost pre-Raphaelite.

Now every bride wants something different and individual – and it's my job to interpret how they want to look. The dress offers the biggest clue to choosing the flowers; a simple embroidered cotton dress, for example, suggests a country look, where the bouquet should look as if the bride has gathered the flowers herself.

The constraints of an all-white wedding are long gone: these days a winter bride feels perfectly at ease wearing red velvet, while a beach wedding on a Caribbean island is even more informal. I'd say about 90 per cent of the bridal flowers we put together today at the shop are tied bouquets; they're much less formal, and look natural and relaxed. The big advantage with a tied bouquet is that you can stand it in water during the wedding breakfast or between photo sessions, to keep it in perfect condition.

Above right **A subtle tied bouquet in shades of green, including hellebores, green and black widow iris and loose pompoms of guelder rose, studded with black ivy berries and silver senecio foliage.**
Right **A handful of fritillaries tied with a ribbon.**
Opposite **Shades of blue in a tied bouquet of hyacinths, forget-me-nots and anemones, with tones of lilac from salvia and lavender flowers.**

This page **A tied bouquet of pink and white roses mixed with scented geranium leaves, swathed in a cloud of tulle for a hazy, romantic effect.**

Opposite **Roses can be bold and vampish, too. Blood red 'Nicole' and 'Black Magic' roses, as intensely coloured as jewels, are wired with red glass beads.**

party headdress

When I opened my flower school at the end of the 1980s, headdresses for brides couldn't have been any heavier, yet we still taught students how to wire a dainty tiara. 'Who on earth would want to wear this?' you could almost hear them groan as they fiddled with the delicate wiring techniques. Girls of today is the answer – one very good reason why it is important to maintain traditional techniques as you never know when you're going to need them.

This headdress is a simpler, less contrived idea than a bride's tiara. It's a perfect party accessory that fits with the current trend for beading, embroidery, satin and chiffon. And, of course, it would make a pretty bridesmaid's circlet. A headdress of fresh flowers has to be made on the day of the celebration. Keep it cool and damp until it's needed. Always have a practice run a day or two before the big day so that you feel confident of the technique.

1 Hyacinths are ideal for a headdress as their waxy flowers last well. Strip the florets carefully from the hyacinth stems. I find the easiest way to do this is to pinch them off with my fingernails, but you can use scissors, if you prefer.

2 Cut a length of wire slightly longer than the widest part of the head, or just over twice as long if you plan to encircle the head a couple of times. Make a hook at one end by folding the wire into a loop and twisting the end round to bind it in place.

3 Thread the hyacinth florets on to the wire. Push the wire vertically through the base of each floret, so that it is held centrally on the wire. Make sure the florets all face in the same direction so that they sit snugly inside each other.

4 Add some beads, just as if you were stringing a necklace. Try to follow a vague pattern: here I've used two to three florets followed by six or seven beads, sometimes varying the bead design.

5 Finally, when the wire is full of florets and beads, twist the end into a simple hook to fasten to the loop you made earlier.

materials

1 or 2 stems of hyacinth
  flowers
fine silver florist's wire
  (36 gauge)
assortment of beads

alternative flowers
agapanthus, delphiniums,
stocks

3

table decorations

For years we were used to hotel or restaurant dining tables decorated with traditional round posies, rigidly set in florist's foam; they looked the same wherever you went, just as if they'd been churned out of a mould. Nowadays eating out – or at home – tends to be much more informal. Foods go in and out of favour, as does the way dishes are presented, and, accordingly, florists have kept up with modern chefs, adopting different styles and techniques to suit.

The setting will often determine the style of table decoration. For an informal supper at the kitchen table, simple glass vases or jam jars would be appropriate; similarly, in a country kitchen, terracotta pots, left natural or painted, could be filled with flowers. For a grander, more traditional dinner, there's no need for a formal centrepiece – a relaxed flower arrangement can still look special. Imagine a crystal bowl filled with water and floating flowers, beautiful enough to grace the grandest table.

far-eastern flowers

This oriental table setting is a real budget arrangement. By adding cherry blossom stems to the green tea bottles, you can't fail to notice the oriental allusion. When cherry blossom is out of season, substitute snake grass or single stems of orchids. You can use the same principles for different menus: tequila bottles and glory lilies for a Mexican evening, or informal place mats torn from Arabic newspapers for a Middle-Eastern feast – but make sure you won't offend any guests who may be able to read the headlines.

floating flowers

It's a fact of life: we can have the best intentions but, before we know it, we run out of time to do anything remotely complicated. So here's my solution for the fastest table setting ever. It's also ideal if you don't want the decoration to look too contrived. Take any dishes, fill them with water and float flowers, or just their petals, on top. If you do have time to plan ahead a little, try to use contrasting colours, such as the blue bowls and pink petals shown here.

candle garland

Here's something for a grander occasion: a candle centrepiece with a new twist that makes it look bang up to date. Gone are the overfamiliar tapered candles or white church pillars, to be replaced by one gigantic candle in a rich shade of chocolate brown; I sometimes wonder if candles can get any bigger. A ring of carnations encloses the candle, and a toning wire-and-petal garland snakes the length of the table. The carnations are pressed into a wreath base traditionally used for funeral work but equally effective at the table. It has a plastic base that protects whatever surface it stands on.

1 **To make the garland, pull out the petals from the carnation and gerbera heads. Cut about 2m (6¹/₂ft) of craft wire. I used two techniques to fix the petals to the wire, to add interest to the finished garland, sometimes threading them on to the wire and other times just twisting the wire round the petals to hold them in place. Add the petals in clusters of five or six, and space them out, knotting or twisting the wire in between so that it will catch the candlelight.**

2 **Fill a bowl or the sink with water and float the wreath base on top, with the plastic base uppermost; this is the part that protects the tabletop from spillages, once it's been dried. Don't try to push the wreath underwater as you may get an airlock. It takes minutes to soak.**

3 **To decorate the wreath, cut the remaining carnation stems very short, so that each stem is about 2.5cm (1in) long, as the calyx (the green base of the flower) is quite deep and holds the flower away from the wreath. For an even finish, start adding flowers around the outside edge. Then fill in the inner edge and, finally, the top of the wreath.**

materials

5 carnation heads for the
    garland
5 gerbera heads for the
    garland
reel of red craft wire
florist's foam wreath with
    integral plastic base
60–80 carnation heads for the
    wreath

alternative flowers
chrysanthemums, zinnias,
pinks, cornflowers, marigolds

1   2

anemone tumblers

Humble glass tumblers are transformed into
something special by dressing each one in a
dracaena leaf. Cut off the stems, then wrap
the leaves around the tumblers, pinning them
in place with cocktail sticks. Other leaves
to try include aspidistra or hosta, and if you
choose leaves with twiggy stems, you can use
these in place of cocktail sticks. If you can't
find leaves large enough to encircle the glass
completely, wrap a band of double-sided
sticky tape horizontally around the glass and
press five or six upright magnolia or laurel
leaves firmly against the tape. Tie them in
place with ribbon, cord or raffia, depending
on the setting. Finally, gather the anemones
in your hand and trim the stems short and
level, gauging them against the tumbler, so
that the heads sit on the rim of the glass.

Using leaves to cover a container

is a favourite trick of mine. Here a single dracaena leaf has been wrapped around each tumbler, its purple brush strokes of colour echoing the hue of the anemones above.

fruit & flowers

Combining fruit and flowers in an arrangement is nothing new – think of the paintings by the 17th-century Dutch masters. More recently, in the 1980s, they were put together in a very literal, realistic way: rustic baskets of apples and cabbages mixed with sweet william, for example. I've moved the whole idea on a stage by using fruit and flowers together in a contemporary setting, and also by using clashing colours. This arrangement would suit a buffet table; it's much too tall for a conventional dining table.

materials

blocks of florist's foam
about 25 carnations
about 25 roses
about 25 poppies
about 5 arum lilies
about 16 tangerines
bundle of small narrow
    garden canes
about 12 stems of rhubarb for
    the outer vase decoration,
    plus extra leaves for the
    central arrangement
bundle of medium-gauge
    (71 gauge) florist's wires
double-sided sticky tape
length of thin cord

1 **Cut several blocks of florist's foam to stand inside the vase – this vase is about 45cm (18in) high – and pile them up so that the top block sits about 10cm (4in) above the rim. This allows you to angle some stems upwards, to make a dome shape.**

Cut all the flower stems down to about 8–10cm (3–4in) and impale the tangerines on garden canes, cut to a similar length. Alternatively, you could reuse the discarded flower stems to stake them. Cut some rhubarb leaves from the stems and twist a length of wire round each one to make a stem that can be pushed into the foam. Start to make the arrangement by adding elements in a straight line across the centre of the block, then make another line at right angles to the first before filling in the four quarters, to keep a neat domed effect.

2 **Add flowers and fruits in small groups rather than dotting them randomly, to give a more recognizable pattern to the arrangement.**

When the florist's foam is completely covered, finish by adding the rhubarb stems to the exterior of the vase. Fix a band of double-sided sticky tape horizontally around the vase, about three-quarters of the way up, and press the stems firmly against the tape. Use another rhubarb stem horizontally to hide the tape, fixing it to every other upright stem with short lengths of cord tied in a simple knot.

fiesta flowers

I love to shop in supermarkets, both at home and abroad, and I could be called a marketing man's dream. No matter what the contents, it's the packaging – the colour, shape and design – that makes me want to buy.

For this table decoration I've gone to town and used a truly global mixture of colourful tins. I bought the tins in the first place simply because I liked the packaging; the contents were promptly discarded. The fiery reds and yellows – the colour scheme for most of the tins – are picked up by the flowers: multi-coloured red and yellow glory lilies, yellow and red oncidium orchids and zingy orange marigolds, mixed with clear yellow mimosa and amber dendrobium orchids, all suggesting hot spicy food.

The tins were washed thoroughly and then filled with water before the flowers were added. They are placed fairly randomly on the table, although I have tended to position the taller flowers towards the centre.

I've played up the colour scheme even further by using a packet of boldly coloured Japanese origami paper, spreading the sheets on the table in place of a cloth, for an extra vibrant effect. The overall table setting is fairly simple, yet it really causes a stir.

flower bowls

I love the idea of encasing flowers in a container; it's such a complete contrast to standard arrangements. Another aspect of these flower bowls is the play on food. I've set the flowers in typical Japanese and Chinese rice bowls, and they look delicious. You can take the allusion still further by adding incense sticks as fantasy chopsticks.

The flowers I've used are carnations, 'Paper White' narcissi, poppies, amaryllis and gerbera. All the flowers are sitting straight in water but on very short stems. If you want to add incense sticks, just slot them in between the flowers, which are so densely packed that they'll hold them firmly.

As well as using full gerbera heads, I've stripped others of their outer petals, to leave the interesting, textured centres – a good way of making use of flowers past their best.

I adore having flowers around me all the time. While I love extravagant or unusual arrangements for special occasions, I'm equally fond of everyday flowers – maybe just a couple of stems on the kitchen windowsill. You don't need masses and masses of flowers for day-to-day decoration at home; they shouldn't leap out at you and be the first thing you notice when you enter a room. Choose those that you love and that reflect your personality, but match them to their surroundings, too. In a minimalist interior, half a dozen lilies without foliage are as pared down as you can get, suiting a streamlined setting. In a less orderly interior, something more opulent would be appropriate. You can gauge the effects of both types of designs on the following pages. Shown opposite is a magnificent banana stem, as intricate and detailed as a piece of art. Yet here it is leaning against the hall wall where the family kick off their shoes – the ultimate in casual chic.

hydrangea wreath

This wreath has an appealing simplicity about it. It's well worth making, as the flowers will gradually dry on the wreath, giving it a whole new life as a dried arrangement later in the year. If you have a hydrangea bush in your garden, you can make the wreath quite inexpensively. If not, hydrangeas are on sale as cut flowers from late summer. Ready-made wreath bases like this one are made from two circles of wire, one slightly larger than the other, linked by a supporting wire framework. Once the sphagnum moss is in place, you can't see the frame at all. Moss is sold in garden centres, as a lining for hanging baskets.

1 **Tie the end of the string securely to the wreath base. Shape a couple of handfuls of sphagnum moss into a sausage. Lay the sausage shape on to the wreath and bind it on tightly with the string.**

2 **Keep the string on the reel and tug the reel sharply towards you so that the string really bites into the moss. If the string is too loose, the moss will fall out when you hang up the wreath.**

3 **Repeat the technique until the wreath is covered with moss. Cut the string from the reel, leaving enough to knot it tightly round the wreath and to make a hanging loop.**

4 **Tidy the moss with a pair of scissors, so that you end up with a smooth, rounded effect.** ▷

materials

ready-made wire wreath base,
  25, 30 or 35cm (10, 12 or
  14in) in diameter
reel of garden string
bag of sphagnum moss
bundle of florist's wires, ideally
  90 gauge
10–20 hydrangea heads,
  depending on their size

5 Take a handful of florist's wires – ideally, these should be 90 gauge – from the bundle and cut them in half. These are to make into pins to hold the hydrangea heads firmly in place on the wreath.

6 To shape the cut pieces of wire into pins, which look rather like old-fashioned hair pins, hold each wire so that its mid-point is over the lower scissor blade. Shape it down firmly over the blade for a nice sharp bend, and then lift it off. You'll need to make about 40 pins in total.

7 Hook a pin through the lower stems of a hydrangea head, then hold the head in your hand so that the florets are closely packed together.

8 Start by adding hydrangea heads around the outside edge of the wreath. Lay each head sideways on against the moss, rather than sitting it flat on top, and pin the head down through the stems. You may need to add another pin to hold it firmly in place. Pack the heads close together. That way, even if they wilt they won't flop because each head is supported by its neighbours. Then add hydrangea heads to the inside edge of the wreath; you may need to split the heads up into smaller pieces to allow you to do this neatly. Finally, fill in the top of the wreath.

There's no need to water the wreath; the flowers will slowly dry out, often changing colour as they do so. While lurid pink hydrangeas may not be your ideal colour choice, they will fade to a subtle grey, tinged with magenta; blue heads will turn into muted shades of lavender.

You can use the technique described here to make wreaths for all occasions. I can picture a perfect wedding wreath for the church door, made from white hydrangeas and frothy gypsophila.

Many people, quite rightly, associate wreaths with funerals. But as they are a symbol of eternity – a never-ending circle – they are also perfect for other celebrations, such as weddings and Christmas. In America autumn wreaths are popular, too.

poppies

I love poppies. They are flowers that benefit from being displayed singly, giving you the chance to appreciate their every detail, from the bristly stems to the egg-shaped buds and the crumpled tissue-paper petals before they burst open. There's a wildness about them, too, a refusal to conform; their stems droop and twist and do their own thing. Despite their fragility they have a good lifespan, and they are among the flowers that when bought in bud are practically guaranteed to open. Here, for the price of four poppies, you have an understated yet arresting arrangement that tones with the colour of the walls, while the wrinkled flowers echo the crackle-glaze vases.

topiary tree

materials

20 stems of 'Paper White'
  narcissi
leather shoelace
glass container for water
mesh bag

alternative flowers
yellow narcissi, such as 'Soleil
d'Or', pinks, sweet williams,
amaryllis

I've been making narcissi 'trees' for a long time now. Every spring, when the narcissi come into the shop, I think about doing something else with them, but I always end up making these – they're easy to do and the stems lend themselves to a trunk effect.

Flowers with smooth straight stems are essential, and any leaves on the stems must be stripped off. If multi-flowered stems are used, the flowers should radiate from a single point at the top of the stem, like amaryllis, as their flowers interlock to form a compact ball.

Try to match the cord you tie round the flowers to the containers. I've partnered these semi-transparent mesh bags with a length of leather shoelace; if you are using terracotta pots, for example, twine would look good. Incidentally, these mesh bags conceal glass containers full of water.

1 Unwrap and untie the narcissi and pick up one or two stems. Build up the topiary tree by adding a stem at a time. Add some at slightly lower levels until you are happy with the size and the shape of the dome of flowers.

2 Once you've finalized the shape, tie the stems together. Either tie them close to the flower heads so that the binding won't be seen or, as here, tie them decoratively lower down the stems. I've used a length of leather shoelace, the sort with a square cross-section. Then cut the stems so that they are level and the flowers stand upright in the container. If they still won't stand up straight on their own, wedge them in position with bubble wrap, cellophane or pebbles.

arum lilies

Although lilies, in particular longiflorum lilies, have been rather overused – a cliché from the 1980s – arum lilies have kept some of their exclusivity. Although they've been popular with florists for decades – they were often used as wedding flowers during the 1920s – their strong graphic shapes are ideal for a clean, contemporary setting. Here they've been bound just below the flower heads, topiary style, with a long narrow leaf, flexible enough to tie in a simple slip knot. The cobalt-blue glass vase is a perfect colour match for the circle on the wall – practically the only splashes of colour in the room.

delphiniums

Repetition is the element that gives these delphiniums a modern edge. It's a simple arrangement: four matching vases, each with a stem of 'Blue Bee' delphiniums in a strong shade of blue that looks almost artificial. The colour is the statement: blue flowers in blue vases. It's an arrangement that would work equally well on a mantelpiece, even on a long dining table, as the vases take up minimal space and wouldn't obscure the view across the table.

tropical colour

I've always found tropical flowers rather brash, so I've tried to develop ways of using them more discreetly. Cutting them quite short helps – these particular anthuriums are naturally short-stemmed – as does mixing in the subdued earthy tones of the sugar cane. Tropical flowers are usually associated with modern interiors, but these muted colours mean that the arrangement doesn't look out of place in a more traditional room setting.

1 Unwrap the sugar cane and sort it out; it is often sold in a mixture of lengths. If necessary, chop the lengths into more manageable pieces, anything from 20cm (8in) to 60cm (2ft), keeping the variation in size. In this medium-sized glass cylinder, I've used around 10 stems. For a natural look, gather up the stems and stand them vertically in the vase, then take away your hands and allow them to fall randomly against the glass.

2 Then take the croton leaves and add some directly to the arrangement. Don't feel obliged to stand them so that the leaves are above water – I've used them semi-submerged. Roll the remaining croton leaves up into small cylinders and tie in place with a piece of raffia. Submerge these completely below the water.

3 Some of the anthuriums have quite short stems, so I've wired a few of them together, binding in a shorter-stemmed flower halfway down the stem of a longer one. I've used bright orange anthuriums to pick up the colours on the croton leaves, but there are other shades on the market.

4 Finally, tuck the anthuriums into the vase behind the croton leaves so that you can't see their stems; you only want to see the rolled-up leaves and the cane stems below water, not criss-crossing anthurium stems.

materials

bundle of sugar cane,
    available from market stalls
    or Caribbean greengrocers
6 or 7 croton leaves
raffia
9 anthurium flowers
bundle of medium-gauge
    (71 gauge) florist's wires

green peace

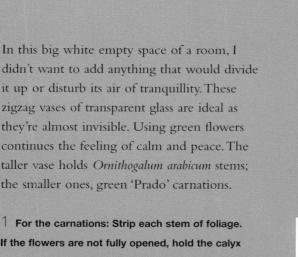

In this big white empty space of a room, I didn't want to add anything that would divide it up or disturb its air of tranquillity. These zigzag vases of transparent glass are ideal as they're almost invisible. Using green flowers continues the feeling of calm and peace. The taller vase holds *Ornithogalum arabicum* stems; the smaller ones, green 'Prado' carnations.

1 **For the carnations: Strip each stem of foliage. If the flowers are not fully opened, hold the calyx in one hand and brush your other hand over the petals. This literally brushes the flowers open by separating the petals. You need to do this to make a nice domed head of flowers.**

2 **Take one central flower and add more stems, building them up in a circle. As you work, pat the heads down into position, to form the shape of the finished dome. You can do this quite firmly with carnations as they are fairly tough, although other species might bruise.**

materials

20 green 'Prado' carnations
   per vase
grey raffia
5 or 6 stems of *Ornithogalum
   arabicum*

alternative flowers
instead of carnations: tulips,
stripped of their leaves; small
alliums; sweet william, for a
multi-coloured effect
instead of *Ornithogalum
arabicum*: agapanthus; small
alliums, still in tight bud

3 **Once you are satisfied with the arrangement, bind the flowers tightly just below their heads with a length of grey raffia; I chose grey raffia because it tones with the greyish-green tinge of the stems. Cut the stems level before binding them close to the ends. Gauge the stems against the vase. I've cut the carnations so that the flowers are just below the rim of the vase, which makes you look twice, to see if the glass is there or not.**

The *Ornithogalum arabicum* stems should also be bound top and bottom with raffia. The flowers illustrated are still in tight bud and, although they will eventually open, for this arrangement I really chose them for their tall straight stems.

Flowers make the perfect gift. They can express a million things that very often we can't bring ourselves to say: I'm sorry; I love you; thanks for everything… But you can't leave it to the flowers alone to convey the message. It has to be backed up by the way they are presented, from the leaves that encircle them to the wrapping paper and the ribbon or string that ties them together. Any one of these accessories can change the impact the flowers have, adding drama or subtlety as needed.

Traditionally, florists' bouquets were flat arrangements, completely encased in a cellophane bag with a backing of thin white paper. When they were unwrapped and displayed in a vase – more often than not, on top of the mantelpiece or sideboard – they formed an uninspiring triangle. Thankfully things have moved on since then, with florists falling over themselves to reinvent the bouquet, following their instincts to create a whole new range of innovative flower designs.

tied tulip bouquet

materials

35–50 tulips
about 14 anthurium leaves
twine
ribbon, cord or a long
   narrow leaf

alternative flowers
roses, gerberas, peonies;
instead of anthurium
foliage, try hosta leaves

The tied bouquet was once called the hostess
bouquet, referring to the fact that the flowers
are arranged so that all the recipient – or
hostess – has to do when she's given the
bouquet is to place it in water. Making a tied
bouquet is quite a difficult technique to
master. It starts with a single central bloom,
around which the subsequent stems are
arranged in a spiral. As the spiral enlarges,
the bouquet takes shape.

   This tied bouquet is a simpler version of
the traditional one, composed of individual
'bunches of five tulips, each wrapped in a large
anthurium leaf, and tied together with twine
to make the final bouquet.

   You'll need around seven small bunches,
made up as follows:

1 **Strip away the excess foliage from the tulips,
otherwise the finished bouquet will be too bulky to
hold. It is particularly important to remove as many
leaves as possible below the binding point of the
finished bouquet – see page 134 for how to work
out the position of the binding point .**

2 **Lay a large anthurium leaf on the work surface
and position five tulips on it centrally. Fold the
lower edges of the leaf inwards and hold it tightly
round the flowers.**

3 **Bind the tulips and leaf together with a length of
twine. Repeat the instructions above to make six
more bunches. ▷**

4

5

6

4 Assemble the individual bunches of tulips into one large bouquet. Hold the first bunch upright and wrap twine round the binding point – about 25cm (10in) below the flower heads – ready to tie in the remaining bunches. Pick up a second bunch.

5 Add the second bunch at a slight angle to the first and bind it in position with the twine. Then hold them in your left hand and rotate the bouquet anti-clockwise before binding in the third bunch.

6 Continue to add the remaining bunches, rotating the main bouquet anti-clockwise before you bind in each one. Eventually all the small bunches will surround the original central bunch. Knot the twine and cut it.

7 Trim all the stems neatly to the same length, using florist's scissors, so that the arrangement will stand upright in the vase.

8 Add an encircling ring of anthurium foliage and bind the leaves in position with twine.

9 & 10 To disguise the twine at the binding point, choose a toning ribbon or cord, or even, as I've used here, a two-tone, long-bladed leaf that can be fastened with a simple but stylish slip knot.

To work out the ideal binding point, you need to have a rough idea of the diameter of your finished bouquet, as the binding point should be half the distance of the diameter below the flower heads. From working with flowers for years, I know that a big bouquet of tulips, such as this, will have a diameter of around 50cm (20in). So, the binding point needs to be 25cm (10in) below the tips of the flowers. You can get a rough idea of the final diameter if you hold all the flowers together before you start to build up an arrangement. The smaller the posy, the closer to the flower heads the binding point needs to be.

This tied bouquet is the perfect gift for someone with no time, or perhaps no skill, to arrange their flowers. Made up of small bunches of tulips, each wrapped in a large anthurium leaf, the finished bouquet requires no unwrapping and can be placed immediately in a vase.

basket of primulas

A basket of brightly coloured primulas could be a traditional, rather staid, spring gift, but here I've turned the idea on its head by using a bold plastic basket instead of a typical wicker one. Any basket needs a plastic liner to protect it from water spills and leaks, but by letting the bright orange plastic liner flounce over the edge of this basket, it has become a feature in its own right.

paper lantern of orchids

A small Chinese paper lantern makes a charming alternative to a wicker basket or sheet of wrapping paper. Hidden inside the lantern is a plastic beaker that holds a small piece of damp florist's foam, to keep the orchids fresh.

antique posy of roses

These exquisite roses have an almost aged appearance. Their extraordinary petals, resembling scraps of antique fabric in an indescribable shade of beigey-pinky-grey, have something of Miss Havisham about them, but without the dust and cobwebs. They deserve a wrapping that complements their air of faded unreality, and a lacy Japanese paper fits the bill perfectly, finished with a ribbon in a suitably subdued shade of pink.

popcorn cone of hyacinths

These indigo-blue hyacinths are bright, sharp and modern, completely in contrast to the roses opposite. I've partnered them with a popcorn-style cone of stiff iridescent card in equally vibrant colours; the whole arrangement shouts out to be looked at. To wrap the flowers, I laid them diagonally on a square of patterned card with the flowers pointing towards one corner, and folded the other corners over. To secure the overlaps, I used double-sided sticky tape.

1

materials

long stem of large green
bamboo

bunches of cut herbs – here
mint and rosemary have
been used, but most smaller
herbs could be substituted,
including thyme, basil,
coriander, marjoram

small pot of lavender

extra potting compost, if
necessary

strands of willow or a hank
of raffia, hemp or twine

medium-gauge (71 gauge)
florist's wire

bay leaf or similar narrow
shiny leaf

herbal offering

A gift of herbs is an ideal present for someone who loves to cook. This arrangement uses pieces of green bamboo cut to length to make three attractive pots. You may have to ask your florist to order the bamboo for you. You'll then need to slice it into shorter lengths with a saw. If you cut it below the leaf nodes – the prominent ridges on the stem – there's a partition in the stem that makes each section a natural container.

1 **Pour water direct into two of the bamboo pots; bamboo is impermeable.**

2 **Strip the lower leaves from the bunches of cut herbs but leave their original bindings in place. If there are no bindings, tie them with a piece of raffia or an elastic band, so that they form a compact shape. Stand a bunch in both pots.**

3 **Remove the lavender plant from its container and repot it in the third bamboo pot. You may need to shake off a little of the soil to fit it in, or you might need to add a little extra potting compost.**

4 **Cut the willow into six long pieces and fasten them together at one end with a short piece of florist's wire. Then plait them, using two stems per plaiting strand, to make an attractive binding for the pots. If your florist doesn't stock willow or can't order it, use raffia or twine instead.**

5 **Fasten the ends of the plait by binding them with another piece of wire.**

6 **Use the willow plait to hold the three pots together, fastening it with a simple slip knot and securing with more wire if necessary. Write your message on a bay leaf and tuck it into the plait.**

Although bamboo pots are not permanent planters, they will last quite a long time, after which the lavender plants can be transferred to the garden.

poppies in bubble wrap

Translucent pink bubble wrap makes a fantastic cushioned covering for these delicate poppies. I've wrapped them parcel-fashion to emphasize the bubble wrap's role in protecting the flowers, and tied it in place with pink wire; as well as picking up the colour, the wire reinforces the industrial note. A single poppy, bound into the knot, makes a pretty finishing touch, and gives a hint of the parcel's contents.

leaf-wrapped orchids

Instead of wrapping these oriental orchids in paper, I chose two dracaena leaves, their undersides echoing the colour of the flowers, in a bid to imitate the way Thai food is often presented. Just as a Thai food parcel comes wrapped in a banana leaf secured with a small twig, so I've used a cut stem to pierce the leaves and hold the arrangement in place. Mimosa foliage highlights the flowers.

The seasons are merging into one; we can now buy tulips in August and strawberries all year round. For me, the miracle of universally available flowers is all the more reason to appreciate the first stocks of summer or the first peonies that no one, as yet, has managed to coax into bloom out of season. And with true seasonal flowers there's always something to look forward to, such as the early snowdrops that indicate spring is on its way. I dread the approach of winter, but then boxes of fragrant pine cones and spicy cinnamon sticks arrive in the shop and Christmas is just around the corner.

Commercially, spring is characterized by yellow and blue – think of daffodils, hyacinths, forget-me-nots – but I like to buck the trend. Shown opposite are flag irises in a rich shade of brown and a brown-stemmed spray of early buds of spiraea. Although the irises are commercially grown, they are on sale for a limited time only, which makes them all the more precious.

spring

**These tall upright
stems of pussy willow
characterize a season
when everything is
shooting into life. The
bundle is standing in
a shallow bowl, so
I've used a traditional
Japanese pin holder
– a lead base studded
with pins, like a bed of
nails, on to which you
push the stems – to
give the bundle stability.
Pebbles disguise the
holder, while a single
length of pussy willow
is woven into a circlet
to hide the binding on
the upright stems.**

summer

**Looking down on to a
bowl of peonies shorn
of foliage forces you
to concentrate on
their colour without
any distractions.
The flowers have been
cut right down and,
breaking with tradition,
packed so tightly
together that they
scarcely show above
the top of the bowl.**

autumn

For me, autumn is about collecting: conkers, dried leaves, berries, acorns, and so on. Here I've used a Perspex desk tray with each compartment half-filled with water to display a collection of interesting objects. There are short lengths of hollow allium stems stood on end, scented geranium leaves tinged with scarlet, late-flowering skimmia in bud, rolled tropical leaves and a stack of reddish twigs laid flat.

winter

Spraying a Christmas tree with fake snow used to be considered naff, but now everything has come full circle; along with lava lamps and all things kitsch, artificial is cool again. A tapering vase layered with glass beads, topped with a miniature Christmas tree frosted with fake snow, sets a suitably icy tone. In case you're wondering, the plant pot is hidden by the beads.

four seasons

Flowers in season are the best buy; they'll be more abundant, in peak condition, and you won't be paying for the hidden costs of air-freighting them in from far-flung locations or for forcing them into bloom in heated glasshouses. See here how one room gains four very different seasonal looks by using only plants and flowers naturally in bloom – or berry – at that time.

spring

Magnolia is such a rarity. It's on sale for a week or two, and then it's gone. To make the most of these boughs, I've set them in modern, galvanized-metal containers, which are so narrow that they hold the magnolia perfectly upright. The vases echo the colour of the walls and don't distract from the flushed-pink flowers. Most spring-flowering magnolias flower before the leaves are produced, giving you the maximum chance to enjoy their magnificent blooms.

summer

Pink can be summery, too. These white ranunculus are faintly flushed with rose, which picks up the pink-tipped buds of the encircling garland of jasmine. White flowers become positively luminescent at dusk, so on a summer evening display them on a side table with a scattering of nightlights. Jasmine also seems to smell even sweeter as night falls. The cut end of the jasmine stem is tucked away in the water.

For a container, I've used a straight-sided glass vase clad in aspidistra leaves, discreetly held in place with double-sided sticky tape, which will last as long as the flowers.

autumn

For an autumnal harvest wreath, you need to take some flexible twigs – willow is ideal, but others will do – and paint them white. Once the paint is dry, form the basic circular shape with two or three twigs and bind them in place with string or wire. If this base is secure enough, the remaining twigs can be woven in without any need for string or wire. Berried stems of *Callicarpa* can be tucked into the wreath and a loop of leather shoelace attached to hang up the finished decoration.

winter

Anemones are cheerful winter flowers, especially in this Christmassy shade of red. The colour is repeated in the early 19th-century decorated milk bottles, which are embellished with red angels advertising egg-nog. Although produced in England, these bottles were exported to the US, and I picked mine up in New York. This arrangement shows how you don't need masses of flowers to create an impact; there are just six anemones displayed here.

flowers, foliage, plants

plant directory

With every trip to market, it seems something new has arrived from some distant exotic place. Importers ring up regularly, wanting to show me new flowers and foliage from all over the world. There are always fresh things to learn, and my style has changed accordingly, in response to this search for novel ideas and ingredients. Customers expect more, too, and I have to live up to their demands.

In this directory I've tried to provide a cross-section of plant ingredients that includes as many of the newest flowers and foliage as possible. Some may not yet be readily available in your local flower shop, but keep asking – they soon will be. I haven't included extras featured in the book, such as conkers or rhubarb, as these are so familiar. Entries are listed alphabetically. The directory is a list of my favourites and not a definitive guide to everything available on the market; they are some of the flowers, foliage and plants I find most exciting right now.

Allium

Alliums sold as cut flowers tend to be the smaller species with heads of tiny white or purple flowers. We also get stems of *Allium giganteum* in season, which, as its name suggests, has enormous flowers. Just one stem in a vase can look sensational, like a flower from outer space. All alliums are members of the onion family and release an oniony smell into the water, which makes it discolour quickly. They also release ethylene, a ripening gas, and other flowers in a mixed arrangement with them won't last as long as normal.

Amaranthus (*Amaranthus caudatus*)

Amaranthus plants were first exported from India during the 16th century. The tasselled flowers are typically rich red in colour, which gives them their common name of love-lies-bleeding, although there is a variety that has striking lime-green flowers. I used red amaranthus in my own wedding bouquet, and I love the way they drape, like crushed velvet. You can let them tumble from their container into a pool on a tabletop, to link the flowers and the surface they're standing on.

Anthurium (*Anthurium andraeanum*)

These flowers are a type of lily, imported all year round from the West Indies. They belong to the same family as our native wild arum lilies. The coloured heart-shaped flower is known as a spathe and the central 'tail' as a spadix. The flowers are amazingly shiny and come in all colours, from pink to brown, white to green. They are also very good value and should last three to four weeks in water. Anthuriums are also sold as house plants and are long-lived in the right conditions, provided the temperature doesn't fall much below 18°C (65°F). The foliage, too, is sold at market; the big glossy leaves are ideal for mixing with other flowers or for wrapping round containers. Some of the leaves are also beautifully variegated – splashed with white or cream.

Aloe vera

Pot plants are back in fashion again after they peaked in the 1970s, and cacti and succulents are some of the trendiest you can buy. Aloes are resilient plants and I love the grey bloom this species has on its thick fleshy leaves. The way the leaves are arranged gives it an interesting outline that looks great in modern apartments.

Amaryllis (*Hippeastrum*)

Amaryllis are native to South America. Their large blooms with fleshy petals are held on thick tubular leafless stems. Seasonal flowers, on sale from November to May either as cut flowers or as pot plants in bud, they come in shades of pink, peach, white and red, and even red- and white-striped varieties. If you grow your own amaryllis as indoor bulbs, you'll have even more colours to choose from. Mini amaryllis are the latest development from flower breeders. If you buy cut flowers in tight bud, they will last for more than two weeks.

Artichoke (*Cynara cardunculus*)

These enormous purple thistles are exactly the same as the artichokes on sale at your greengrocers; the only difference is that the flowers have been allowed to mature, and you certainly wouldn't want to eat them once they're in full bloom. The thistles are proper seasonal flowers, available only in the summer. Their foliage is wonderful, too: great sculptural arching leaves that are soft and downy on the undersides, but painfully spiny along the margins.

Anemone

Anemones have upright cup-shaped flowers in a range of jewel colours, with contrasting sooty-black stamens. When I first started work anemones were tiny and available only in multi-coloured bunches. Over the years I've seen them mature, so that now they are almost a different flower: long-stemmed and sold in single colours.

Aspidistra (*Aspidistra elatior*)

Aspidistras were once synonymous with respectability, symbolizing the etiquette of the parlour in Victorian days. For years they were reviled as boring and old-fashioned plants, but style dictators have lately reappraised them and the leaves are now deeply fashionable for the oriental air they lend to flower arrangements. Dutch growers can supply the leaves all year round as cut foliage. Aspidistra's alternative name of cast-iron plant suggests that it can tolerate just about every physical insult you may wish to throw in its direction, and, indeed, they are extremely tough plants. If you want an aspidistra as a house plant, look out for the variegated variety with leaves striped with white.

Banana plant (*Musa*)

If you want to cause a stir, ask for a stem of a banana plant, complete with tiny bunches of bananas, from your local flower shop. You'll more than likely need to place an order for one as they are not yet widely available. They are also expensive but you do get your money's worth, both in shock value and in longevity, as a stem will last a month or more in water. You can grow banana plants in a warm conservatory, provided the temperature doesn't drop below 10°C (50°F), and it's not unheard of for them to fruit.

Bells of Ireland (*Molucella laevis*)

Green flowers have always been considered sophisticated, by both gardeners and flower arrangers. The green flowers are, in fact, large conical calyces that enclose a tiny, almost insignificant, true flower. They have a strong herbal fragrance that I particularly like. Stems of bells of Ireland work well in mixed arrangements as an additional foliage plant. Put them with aspidistra leaves for an oriental look, mass them with larkspur and scabious for a cottage-garden grouping, or keep them on their own for an equally dramatic effect. The flowers can also be dried, although they lose their colour. You're bound to spot them in garden borders from time to time, as they're easy-to-grow annuals.

Bamboo

Bamboo, a member of the grass family, has only recently become available commercially as a cut plant. A native of Japan and China, it has, like the aspidistra, a very contemporary oriental appeal. Cut bamboo lasts a long time in water and it can also be used to surround arrangements, for example, by binding lengths of it on to a container. Most species have hollow stems or canes, which can be black, brown, pink, purple or yellow, and sometimes mottled or streaked. I like to strip off the leaves to show the canes to best advantage. Some species grow quite happily in the garden.

Banksia

These amazing plants were discovered in the 18th century by the great naturalist and explorer Sir Joseph Banks, who accompanied Captain Cook on his voyage to Australia. Banksia have a prehistoric fascination about them: you either love them or you hate them, but either way you can't be indifferent to such extraordinary flowers. They have thick woody stems and heavy heads, and look wonderful displayed in massive stoneware vases. The flowers are incredibly textural; this one reminds me of a woolly hat.

Bird-of-paradise (*Strelitzia reginae*)

These native South African flowers are available pretty well all year round, and their long stems and curious architectural flowers make them ideal for modern interiors. The flowers open in succession, as each one finishes, and you can nudge them along by pulling open the next flower with your fingertips as the last one dies. Just work your fingers down into the 'beak' and wiggle the flower out – it's held in a sappy sort of gel.

Carnation (*Dianthus*)

Carnations have suffered a bad press similar to chrysanthemums. When I opened my first shop on St James's Street in London's West End, I didn't sell either of the flowers, and swore that I never would. Now that, many years later, growers have reinvented carnations, giving them green flowers, even terracotta ones, and fringing their petals elaborately, I've had to backtrack and admit I actually like them, even though it's on a par with admitting to wearing flares again. I love their scent, too, which is strongest in the white blooms, and is a clue to the fact that they are closely related to heavily scented garden pinks and sweet william.

Cherry blossom (*Prunus*)

Sprays of early cherry blossom mean spring is on its way; they are also meant to represent a blossoming friendship. For the shop we can buy thin straight stems that have no foliage on them, but I prefer branches cut from an orchard, with knotted gnarled bark and heavy with flowers. Cherry blossom is a true seasonal ingredient, and I wouldn't have it any other way.

Chincherinchee (*Ornithogalum thyrsoides*)

These cup-shaped flowers are extremely long-lasting and available all year round. A pyramid of buds is held on a tall straight stem. I like the combination of bright white flowers and green stem, which is very easy to work with.

Chrysanthemum (*Dendranthema*)

Like carnations, spray chrysanthemums have had an image problem over the past few years. They've become synonymous with supermarket flowers, available all year round and with little else to commend them. But they're back in fashion and have been reinvented with some startling new colours, such as green and brown. The big-headed varieties are another story altogether. Their splendid flower heads massed with petals are classified according to their shape, such as 'incurved', 'reflexed', 'pompom' and 'spider'. Originating in China, where they were considered noble plants,

Celosia

Some species of celosia have plumes of feathery or grass-like flowers, but my favourite is *Celosia argentea* (pictured), which I think has a lovely texture, resembling velvet ribbon – although some people say it reminds them of a brain. When combined with other flowers, celosia gives them a sumptuous background, especially if you cut the celosia shorter, so that it is lower in the arrangement and appears to weave through the longer stems.

Chinese lantern (*Physalis alkekengi*)

Chinese lanterns are another garden species popular as cut flowers. The lanterns, produced in autumn, are really a type of papery seed case that protects the single orange berry inside each one. They retain their characteristic orange colour even when dried. I like to arrange them alongside pumpkins and gourds for a fantastic Halloween display.

together with the plum, bamboo and orchids, chrysanthemums were introduced into Japan in the fourth century, and figure heavily in ancient textile designs and other artworks. They have just about the longest lifespan of any cut flowers, lasting three to four weeks, provided the water is changed regularly. As soon as I smell their unmistakable fragrance, I am transported back to my first job in a workroom in Essex, where I had to wire thousands of chrysanthemums for funeral wreaths. The bronze flowers are said to symbolize friendship; red ones, love; and white, truth.

Croton

Another 1970s' throwback, the croton was one of the first tropical house plants to hit these shores. Soon its dark green leaves, splashed with bright red, orange and yellow variegations, were seen everywhere but, as the old saying goes, familiarity breeds contempt and the croton eventually fell from favour. Now it's back, but as cut foliage and in great demand for modern tropical arrangements.

Dracaena

Familiar for years as a house plant, the narrow grass-like leaves of dracaena are becoming indispensable in modern oriental arrangements. They come in a variety of hues, with soft brush strokes of colour ranging from lime green to aubergine. They are very long-lasting in water, and are also good to wrap round containers.

Eleagnus

Eleagnus has small neat evergreen foliage that is useful for bouquets or for mixing with cut flowers. Some species have leaves variegated with gold, some are silvery, while others are dark with silvery undersides. In winter there's an added bonus, as it produces tiny white bell-shaped flowers that are highly perfumed.

Eucalyptus

There are hundreds of different varieties of eucalyptus, and they're not just sold for their foliage; you can buy stems with seed pods and even flowering branches. The foliage is highly scented, and after a day working with eucalyptus in the shop I can smell it on my hands for hours afterwards. When I was 15 I persuaded my dad to buy a eucalyptus tree for the garden because I'd been inspired by working with the foliage in my Saturday job at the local florists. It's the bane of his life now as it has never stopped growing.

Delphinium

Delphiniums make magnificent cut flowers. The tall Elatum varieties come in shades ranging from deepest indigo to pastel pink via iridescent blue. Belladonna delphiniums have branching flower stems and looser, more relaxed flower spikes. I love the dainty, pointed flower buds and I never discard the sideshoots for this reason. They are such romantic, typically English flowers, and even some of the cultivar names, such as 'Lancelot' and 'Guinevere', are evocative.

Delphiniums have hollow stems prone to air bubbles. One trick is to hold a cut flower upside down and fill the stem with water. Then hold your thumb over the end and quickly stand the flower the right way up in a vase of water.

Eryngium (*Eryngium planum*)

Eryngium are available from florists nearly all year round now. Some varieties have intensely blue flowers, while others are more silvery grey, and they vary in size, too. They are also splendid garden plants, and although they will only be in bloom from mid- to late summer the flowers can be dried successfully. The leaves and the ruffs that surround the flowers are spiny, but the stems of the cut flowers are not too difficult to handle.

Euphorbia

This is a large family of plants, with flowers ranging from lime green to flame-coloured, particularly in the summer-flowering species. Others have foliage that becomes red-tinged later in the year. One of the commonest cut-flower euphorbias is *Euphorbia fulgens*, which comes in red, white, orange and purple varieties. All euphorbias have a sticky white sap that can irritate sensitive skins. Christmas poinsettias are members of the same family.

Forget-me-not (*Myosotis*)

These pretty flowers are available in spring, and spring only. Although they don't have a very long lifespan once cut, their cottage-garden-appeal is irresistible. They are easy-to-grow garden plants and do well in light shade; once you've got them, they tend to come up year after year. Pink- and white-flowered varieties are available, as well as the classic blue. Their symbolism is obvious from the name, attributed to a medieval knight, dying in battle, who threw a posy to his lover, crying out, 'Forget me not'.

Fritillary (*Fritillaria meleagris*)

I love the snake's head fritillary. It's one of the smaller species and is on sale only in spring. The flower stems are completely uncontrollable – they twist all over the place – but I like that, the unexpected, when flowers refuse to conform and retain some of their wild character. Snake's head fritillaries used to grow in profusion in water meadows in southern England, and there are still a few protected sites where you can see them today. Taller members of the family – crown imperials, for example – have a curious smell, almost sulphur-like. I adore it, but I know that it's not everyone's cup of tea.

Gerbera

Gerberas are modern extrovert flowers. They were popular for years then suffered something of a backlash, and just when I thought I couldn't bear to look at another gerbera, plant breeders reinvented fashion's fallen idol. They've given it crazy petals, which look as though someone's attacked them with a pair of scissors, and extended its palette to include the most outrageous shades, from Barbie pink to brown. Even the central eye of the flower hasn't escaped the face lift and can now be brown, black or cream, or even a rosette of tightly packed green petals.

Freesia

These are traditional bridal flowers and probably will continue to be so, because of their delicate fragrance and also because their waxy petals resist drooping. Freesias come in pinks, blues and yellows as well as white and – the very latest shade – brown. Double-flowered varieties are also available. The wide range of commercial varieties means that we can buy freesias of one kind or another all year round, whereas garden-grown plants bloom only during the summer months.

Geranium, scented

The flowers of scented geraniums are minuscule and hardly worth mentioning, but the fragrance of their leaves is something else. You can choose from lemon to rose, mint to chocolate, and many others in between. Some of the leaves have interesting markings or a soft hairy texture, while others are beautifully shaped, resembling oak leaves, or deeply cut.

Gladiolus

The much-maligned gladiolus, for ever linked to Dame Edna and to unimaginative soldier-like rows in the garden, can look stunning in the right situation. Left really tall and massed in a dramatic vase, their impact is astounding. You can even buy wonderful green gladioli, a variety called 'Woodpecker', which has a dark red eye. Maybe there's a grower out there who'll do further work to make them even more exciting.

Grasses

In the past few years, grasses have become enormously fashionable, both as cut flowers and for growing in the garden. There are so many different varieties, ranging from small, compact scirpus grass – which makes an ideal pot plant – to the strong blades of steel grass, striped with green and grey. As well as additions to arrangements, grasses are great for wrapping round containers, to transform an uninspiring vase into something more interesting. Narrow grasses can be used in place of raffia to bind flowers; wider grasses can be tied round a bunch instead of ribbon. Grasses of some sort are on sale all year round.

Guelder rose (*Viburnum opulus* 'Roseum')

Green flowers are among my favourites, and I love the compact heads of these tiny flowers that open out into almost-perfect spheres – hence their other common name, the snowball bush. Their greenish tinge is useful for reinforcing touches of green in other flowers or in foliage. Guelder roses are often used as 'fillers', beneath or in between other flowers, but they are rarely the star of the show.

Golden rod (*Solidago, Solidaster*)

When I first started work, golden rod was a seasonal flower that wasn't grown commercially; we had to buy it direct from garden growers and smallholders. Now it's available all year round, and its fluffy yellow sprays compete with gypsophila as a popular 'filler' plant in supermarket bunches. In the Victorian language of flowers, golden rod is said to represent indecision.

Grape hyacinth (*Muscari*)

These small spring flowers have compact spikes of flowers in shades of blue, from inky to pale sky, as well as in white. There's a nice contrast between the leafless lime-green stems and the fresh blue flowers. I still get really excited when I go to market and the first boxes of the season arrive. In some ways I long for the season to be extended so that grape hyacinths would become more available, but at the same time I know that they would lose their edge. Grape hyacinths are ideal flowers to place on a bedside table.

The taller varieties make a superb display on their own; there's really no need to add flowers. They are very long-lasting in general, and can often be dried in the vase. Take care when working with grasses, as some of the tougher ones can cut your hands.

Gypsophila

The pick of the garage forecourt bunch has somehow lost its value along the way. Its tiny white florets on fine hair-like stems made it a favourite 'filler' to use with roses; it creates a lovely cloud around stronger flowers. I have to confess I seldom use it in this way now, although I have been experimenting with its hazy qualities in other ways. I once used gypsophila for a 'heavenly' theme, producing a wonderful cloud-like effect with enormous topiary trees. It's equally useful fresh or dried, and is available all year round. Gypsophila is also very easy to grow in the garden.

Hellebore

A lovely greeny-white shade, hellebores are all the more precious because they are on sale for only a very short time in spring. Traditional white Christmas roses belong to the hellebore family. They are grown commercially but are very expensive. The later spring-flowering oriental species, in antique shades of purple and pink, have a vintage look, like flowers from another era. They are meant to signify lies and deceit.

Heliconia

Heliconias were one of the first tropical flowers on the scene. The first species to reach these shores were great brash flowers in a vivid shade of pink – not an instant hit with me. Flown in from the West Indies, they now come in subtler shades and shapes, including yellow and white. Occasionally they are referred to as ginger lilies.

Hyacinth (*Hyacinthus orientalis*)

Bulb flowers, such as hyacinths, are fashionable at the moment. I love their fragrance, and especially the blue or white flowers, although they come in colours from pink to cream, salmon and apricot, with the occasional striped variety. I almost prefer them before they are fully in bloom, in that organic bud stage. Their one disadvantage is that the cut stems ooze a sticky slimy sap. Although I adore them as cut flowers or pot plants, I don't like them in the garden – they look too park-like, somehow.

Iris

Modern-day Dutch bulb irises – typically white, yellow and purple – have lost some of their charm for me, mainly because they are available all year round. But I can't get enough of the widow iris (*Hermodactylus tuberosus*) (pictured); I adore its green flowers with their bumblebee splash of black velvet. Unlike its more commonplace relatives, the widow iris is on sale for only a short period in spring. We are now starting to see flag irises grown commercially, which I'm really excited about. It's still early days yet, but we can buy flag irises with wonderful chocolate-brown petals, for example, as well as classic purple.

Herbs

I've always liked the idea of including fragrant foliage with flowers, especially if the flowers themselves are unscented. Herbs tie in nicely with our growing awareness of aromatherapy: rosemary (pictured) can be uplifting while eucalyptus is positively invigorating. Rosemary was a traditional bridal foliage, symbolizing remembrance; humble garden mint indicates homeliness; and marjoram means modesty. Stems of spiky-leaved rosemary are also useful for adding texture to an arrangement. The foliage is evergreen, so is always available, and the underside of the leaves are a contrasting silvery-grey. The flowers are a purple-blue.

Hydrangea

Hydrangeas originally came from Japan but are now well established in our gardens. They have only recently become popular as cut flowers; at one time we had to buy them in as pot plants and cut the flowers off to use. Hydrangeas are ideal for wedding work and are extremely versatile. As fresh flowers they will last about a week in water but they can be dried by leaving them in water as the flowers gradually fade; if you don't keep them in water as they dry, they won't always retain a firm stem and shape. Alternatively, preserve the flowers by leaving them on the bush until almost dry, then finishing them off in a dark cupboard.

Ivy (*Hedera*)

Ivy is one of my favourite foliage plants, simply because of the huge range available, from great flat-leaved species to the tiny 'Needlepoint' variety, which is ideal for brides' posies. Many ivies come in variegations of yellow, light green, white, silver and even red. Now they are grown commercially, but supplies used to come from foliage merchants who would go out into the countryside or to large gardens to cut ivy and other leafy plants. If supplies were short, we sometimes had to buy pot plants and cut them down. I remember once creating a 3.7m (12ft) trail of ivy for a bride, which she wore in place of a train. It's an apposite bridal foliage as its clinging nature is said to represent the bond between husband and wife.

Kangaroo paw (*Anigozanthos*)

These flowers are imported from Australia and are gradually becoming more widely available commercially. The tall stems bear clusters of flowers in shades of orange, red and greeny-yellow, and both flowers and stems are smothered in soft black bristles. The bristles stand out wonderfully against the greeny-yellow variety, and I love their interesting sooty texture. Kangaroo paws are good value and long-lasting as cut flowers.

Lavender (*Lavandula*)

I love big banks of lavender in a garden, inevitably covered with bees and butterflies in midsummer. It looks glorious indoors or out, and, of course, it dries easily, so can be mixed into pot pourri or sewn into scented sachets. Although lavender is said to signify refusal, its heavenly scent makes it much in demand for brides' and bridesmaids' posies. Flowers vary in intensity from deep purple to pale blue, and there are also pink and white varieties. The foliage is scented, too, and the narrow grey-green leaves can add colour as well as texture to an arrangement.

Lily of the valley (*Convallaria majalis*)

Such is the demand for lily of the valley for weddings that it is now available all year round, forced into flower, but you really do pay for the privilege. It's much better value in its natural season, which is early May. Lily of the valley is also sold as a flowering pot plant, and you can always try digging up a clump from the garden, potting it and bringing it indoors for an early flowering treat. The flowers are meant to be a symbol of friendship.

Kangaroo tail (*Xanthorrhea australis*)

Another Australian import and a real show-stopper. You'll need a large architectural vase to support the enormous stems of kangaroo tail, which can easily be 90cm (3ft) tall. The tall straight flower heads are covered with dense soft brown 'fur', a little like a bulrush, and studded with tiny flower buds that gradually open out into starry flowers. Definitely not a flower for the faint hearted, it needs to be used in big bold displays.

Lilac (*Syringa*)

I remember the lilac tree in my grandmother's garden, and its perfume, which always strikes me as a melancholy fragrance; there's really nothing uplifting about it. If you cut lilac from the garden, it hardly lasts any time at all. Commercially grown varieties have been bred to last longer, but at a price – they are scentless. It seems that the gene that controls fragrance also controls longevity, so you end up sacrificing one for the other.

Lisianthus

Lisianthus is a relatively new cut flower that came on the scene about ten years ago. The flowers come in shades of purple, lilac, pink, cream and white, and as bicolours, for example, white flowers with a lavender rim. The blooms can be single or double, and are long-lasting, but they have never really hit the big time. For me, they're nice but not heart-stoppingly beautiful.

Lily

White longiflorum lilies with their tubular sweet-scented flowers reached their pinnacle in the 1980s, but that doesn't mean to say lilies are past it. A never-ending range of new colours has ensured they stay in the limelight. An elegant favourite of mine is the oriental 'Casablanca' lily, which has wide open flowers and a lovely scent. White lilies, especially the Madonna lily (*Lilium candidum*), have long been associated with purity and the Virgin Mary; they are often used to decorate churches at Easter.

Then there are the streamlined arum lilies (*Zantedeschia aethiopica*) (pictured). Although some people associate them with funerals, they are very popular for wedding bouquets, too. They have been used for both because in the past there just wasn't the choice of flowers we have today. For me, they have that American black-and-white movie-star image, that elegance of the 1920s and 1930s. They are also available in yellow, a tawny orange, pink and – my favourite – white tinged with green. Glory lilies (*Gloriosa superba*), tropical climbing plants from Africa and Asia, have pink and yellow stripes. I like the way the narrow petals of each flower curl right back to reveal stamens shaped like a spinning wheel.

Lotus (*Nelumbo*)

Lotuses are native to Japan. They look – and grow – like water lilies, but we tend to see just the naked seed heads imported here, either fresh and green or dried and brown. If you buy them in the green, they soon dry to brown. In Japan lotus roots are a delicacy for the table; they are known as *hasu* and are served in various dishes, like *sushi*. Very, very occasionally, a box of lotus flowers turns up at market but although I can never resist buying them, I usually regret it as they are notoriously short-lived.

Marguerite (*Argyranthemum frutescens*)

These simple daisy-like flowers are typical of late spring and early summer. They make good cut flowers as well as outdoor pot plants. We sell them trained into classic standards: lollipop-shaped balls of flowers and foliage on top of an elongated bare stem.

Mimosa (*Acacia dealbata*)

Sometimes I feel ambivalent about mimosa. I have to confess that yellow isn't my favourite colour and, combined with the fact that no matter what I do I can't persuade mimosa to last more than a few days, this rather puts me off it. But I do like its wonderful fragrance and the way its fluffy pompoms of flowers cascade down the stem.

Mind-your-own-business (*Soleirolia soleirolii*)

These little foliage plants have become fashionable in the past couple of years. They come in three shades that look very effective grouped together: lime yellow, variegated silver and ordinary green. They can be difficult to look after as indoor plants as they dry out quickly and need misting daily. But let them anywhere near your lawn and you'll soon regret it – there's no stopping them.

Magnolia

Magnolia blossom is seasonal and fleeting. I love the tulip-shaped flowers on bare stems and the way the buds curl back to release the waxy petals. In the garden on a sunny day, when the petals are warm, some magnolia species release a delicate lemony fragrance. Preserved magnolia leaves make useful foliage for winter arrangements, either in their natural glossy green state with their brown suede undersides, or glycerined and dyed in Christmassy shades such as a deep burgundy.

Marigold (*Calendula officinalis*)

The humble cottage-garden marigold has always been a popular cut flower. It comes in single and double varieties, and in a range of colours from cream and apricot to yellow. I love their pungent 'green' fragrance and I always have some growing in my garden; they self-seed quite happily everywhere. The flowers were once attributed with the powers to heal a lovers' tiff, provided they were gathered without speaking and placed on a windowsill. They were supposedly at their most potent on Midsummer's Day.

Narcissus

Narcissi and daffodils are still truly spring flowers, although growers have extended the season a little so that we can buy daffodils at Christmas. The variety 'Paper White' (pictured) was popular with the Victorians, who liked to grow the flowers in pebbles and force them into bloom for Christmas. 'Soleil d'Or' are the golden-yellow variety. Narcissi are named after the beautiful youth who, according to Greek mythology, fell in love with his reflection and pined away, turning into the flower that bears his name. It's no surprise that they have come to symbolize self-love.

Ornamental cabbage

Once popular as pot plants or as edging for garden borders, ornamental cabbages are now sold on long stems for flower arranging. Before this we had to buy them in as pot plants and wire them to canes to give them height. As well as the classic greeny-white cabbage heads, they come in pinks and purples.

Peony

The most appealing thing about peonies is the layer upon layer of petals. I love all the colours they come in, from peach to sugar pink to dusty rose. I found a grower just outside New York who produces about 40 different varieties for the cut-flower trade, but in the UK we are limited to about five. The commonest one on sale is 'Sarah Bernhardt', with ruffled flowers that are slightly scented. In the Victorian language of flowers, including peonies in a bunch of flowers was a way of saying sorry.

Orchid

Advances in growing methods have brought orchids right down in price. Where once breeders had to wait several years for a seedling or cutting to mature and flower, micropropagation techniques now produce flowering plants in a matter of months. Orchids have dipped in and out of fashion; the garish cymbidium flower heads that were sold in a plastic box on Mother's Day did much to cheapen their reputation, but even they have made a comeback. Other popular cut flowers include the moth orchid (*Phalaenopsis*), which has pure white flowers, and the dendrobium orchid, with its sprays of yellow scented flowers. Orchids last and last, and look good in contemporary interiors.

Poppy (*Papaver*)

Poppies are one of my favourite flowers. I even love the buds before they open: fat, hairy cases on bristly, twisted stems. I'm so used to the perfectly straight stems grown commercially that I get excited when I come across something that has retained its individuality, despite the growers' best efforts – it's so refreshing. Try to buy poppies in bud with the colour just beginning to peek out. Poppies last quite well, but the stems begin to rot first, so it's essential to change the water daily, to reduce the chance of this happening.

Primula

The primula family is a large one and my particular favourites have to be auriculas. At the Chelsea Flower Show, I always head straight for the stand where they are shown, displayed against a black-velvet backdrop, with their extraordinary antique flowers of scarlet edged with green, or deep burgundy with a white eye. Common primulas seem rather naïve, like a child's drawing; I like them in window boxes or as pot plants, but in the garden they can look a little municipal.

Protea

It's no surprise that proteas look prehistoric as this family of flowers has been around for 300 million years. Explorers brought them back to Europe from their native Africa in the 16th century. The Empress Josephine grew them as a hobby at her garden at Malmaison. They were named for Proteus, the Greek god who took on many forms, as there are more than 1,400 varieties. The queen protea (pictured) has goblet-shaped flowers filled with soft silky bracts. It is long-lived in water and can be successfully dried; in fact, it will dry naturally if left in a vase, which makes the flowers better value, as they are expensive.

Pussy willow (*Salix caprea*)

The soft furry flowers of pussy willow are produced before the stems burst into leaf, which gives you time to appreciate them. Now that willow is grown commercially, we can buy it in straight stems up to 1.8m (6ft) tall, which look amazing in a vase on their own and make a truly architectural statement. Before it was grown to order, we bought much shorter stems with lots of sideshoots, cut direct from the hedgerow, which created a natural look mixed with lime-green euphorbia and tulips, for example. I still use the shorter variety to achieve this informal garden-style bouquet.

Pyracantha

These well-known garden shrubs can be quite spiny and so are not ideal material for flower arranging, but their intensely coloured and long-lasting berries make them worth the risk. The berries can be scarlet, orange or golden yellow. If you're cutting pyracantha from the garden, do it early in the season or you may find that the birds have beaten you to the berries.

Ranunculus

These extravagant multi-petalled flowers are members of the buttercup family. They have layer upon layer of tissue-paper petals, sometimes forming flowers 5cm (2in) across. Always buy them in tight bud and watch as they unfold and double in size. They should easily last two weeks, and come in pink, red,

yellow or white (which is lovely for wedding bouquets). From November through to spring we can buy Dutch and Italian ranunculus in single-colour bunches on long stems. Then, in summer, the English-grown flowers arrive in short-stemmed, mixed-colour posies. I can't quite decide which style I prefer. You quite often see ranunculus sold as pot plants, too.

Red robin (*Photinia*)

Evergreen red robin is available as cut foliage all year round from Dutch growers, but only the newest spring growth is the familiar vivid red colour that gives the plant its name. For the rest of the year, the leaves are a glossy dark green, with neatly serrated edges, making them look a little like rose leaves. Their high gloss is an important factor when considering texture for an arrangement, especially where you are using a mixture of foliages. Red robin is a

Rose

We think of roses as quintessentially English, yet so much depends on how you use them. Roses on long stems appear very Parisian and chic; cut low and mixed with garden flowers, they look like country flowers. These days roses are available all year round, imported from Colombia, Kenya, Israel, Mexico and Holland. Breeders have increased the range of colours they come in as well, to include sepia browns and washed-out purples. The roses cultivated for sale as cut flowers are rarely available as garden plants, but if you want to match the colour of a cut rose with a shrub, it shouldn't be difficult since there are thousands of rose cultivars on sale to gardeners.

Scabious

These flowers are real cottage-garden stalwarts. When I first started working, scabious were my favourite flower, and I still love the way the little 'knots' in the centre gradually open up. They are one of the flowers that have remained unchanged and unimproved throughout my career. They are small growers' flowers and I'd really miss them if the growers went out of business. Although they're not at the forefront of any current trend, there's definitely still a place for such country flowers.

popular shrub for the garden, and to get the best display of red foliage you need to prune the stems in winter so that they produce plenty of new growth the following spring. There are also some deciduous species, whose leaves turn brilliant orange and red in autumn, and which have showy red berries.

Salvia

The salvias sold as cut flowers are a million miles away from the garish red variety beloved of municipal bedding schemes. Strictly speaking, it's not just the flowers themselves that are coloured, but the leaf-like bracts that surround them as well. I like the intense purple varieties and the dusky pinks best. They're not as yet grown commercially, so they can be hard to come by.

Senecio

I hate this shrub's yellow flowers but love its silver leaves. I'm not alone in my opinion: some eminent gardeners share this view and have been known to go into the garden and snip the buds off before they flower. As silver foliage is useful with blues and pinks, it would be disaster to have yellow along, too. Senecio looks lovely in Christmassy combinations with red or white flowers.

Snowdrop (*Galanthus*)

When I see the first boxes of snowdrops in the market, their tiny stems wrapped in raffia or bound with an ivy leaf, I know I'm looking at a labour of love, not a big-business enterprise. Some are grown in convents, and I imagine the nuns' cold fingers as they gather and bind them, and wonder how long the tradition can last. The snowdrops are so beautiful as they are that we never do anything to them. Snowdrops symbolize renewal and it's clear why, when they flower in the depths of winter.

Stephanotis

The smell of stephanotis always takes me back to my time as a trainee wiring hundreds of tiny florets for the senior florist to make into a bouquet. The flowers' waxy texture means they last well, but they do need wiring because their stems are short. We can buy stephanotis wholesale as bags of florets all ready-cut and ready to wire, or they come as pot plants. Although a traditional wedding flower, they slipped from favour for a while, but they are now making a comeback with the demand for smaller bouquets and headdresses.

Tulip

I love tulips, especially the parrot varieties with their brush strokes of colour that seem to bleed across the petals, but I'm also fond of the long-stemmed French tulips. I like the way that they all optimistically carry on growing in the vase, moving towards the light, and eventually collapse over the edge of the container. Tulips are among the cut flowers that are prone to wilting. If you unwrap a bunch and find the stems are soft and won't support the flowers, follow the treatment described on page 65. A few years ago I had the honour to have a tulip named after me; it's a garden bulb, not a commercial cut variety, with orange lily-shaped flowers and a slight fragrance.

Stachys

The soft downy leaves of stachys are commonly called lambs' ears, for obvious reasons. Plants are not grown commercially, so we need to find a supplier who can track them down in a garden or smallholding, which renders them even more valuable. The silky texture of the leaves makes them popular for bridal work.

Sunflower (*Helianthus annuus*)

Sunflowers come in a range of colours now, not just classic yellow petals with a brown centre. The very newest varieties have brown petals that lend an air of antiquity to an arrangement. Sunflowers are very easy to grow: if you want them for cut flowers, varieties that bear multiple blooms on one plant will be more useful than the traditional single-stemmed sunflowers of childhood.

Veronica

These typical country-garden border flowers
are now grown commercially, but the quality
can be erratic. When it is good, they last well.
Veronicas come in shades of purple, white and
dusky pink, plus a shade of blue that I like
to use for coastal themes; to me, they look
like the sort of flower that might grow beside
a beach. They're not really feature flowers; a
couple of stems in a bud vase can look nice,
but otherwise they're better mixed with others.

Violet (*Viola odorata*)

Violets seem like flowers from another era, that of
Dickensian London when they were sold on street
corners. It obviously takes someone a long time to
pick and bind the small bunches, yet they sell for
so little that they are almost bound to disappear
soon. Violets are not long-lasting, but their chances
can be improved by submerging them in a bowl of
water for a while before arranging them (see page
14). Violets are said to represent modesty.

Zinnia

Zinnias seem quite naïve flowers, probably
because they are sold in multi-coloured bunches,
with every hue and shade mixed together – a crazy
assortment of orange, pink and yellow. But even
these flowers have matured over the years, so that
you can now buy larger-headed green varieties,
plus single-colour bunches on longer stems.

index

Page numbers in italic refer
to illustrations

acknowledgments

Author's acknowledgments

Whenever I begin a book, it's always with a sense of nervous excitement, and when it's over and I've breathed a huge sigh of relief, there's a feeling of sadness as I realize I won't be working with the team again, or at least not straightaway!

I've had great fun working on this book, and I'd like to thank all those (and, believe me, there are many!) who have worked with me. Most importantly, Cath and Lesley, who played such a major role: Cath for her absolutely unbelievably fantastic photography, and for her calmness and laughter that helped us through on the tough days, and Lesley for her wonderful styling, eye for detail and her wicked, wicked sense of humour. And, of course, Alison at Conran Octopus for introducing this talented pair, and for her own drive and commitment to the idea. A huge thank you to Avril who rescued us with her intuitive eye, made sense of our piles of photographs and produced overnight a fantastically designed book; to Sharon, who quickly absorbed my rambling thoughts and, amazingly, made sense of them on paper in exactly (and I mean exactly) the way I had hoped; and to Helen, who calmly and patiently soothed our troubles away by pulling it all together. Thank you.

In addition, I'd like to thank my own team at Jane Packer Flowers for all their help with this project.

Publisher's acknowledgments

The publisher would like to thank the following: LSA International (01932 789721) for the 'Giant Orvieto' glass vases, page 36; the large blue 'Viva' glass vase, page 124; the tall blue 'Achilles' vases, page 125; and the glass 'zigzag' vases, page 128; Habitat (0845 6010740) for the ceramic vases, pages 54–5; Momo, 25 Heddon Street, London W1 (020 7434 4040) for kindly letting us photograph in the restaurant, pages 78–81; Twelve 12 mail order catalogue (020 7686 0390) for the wood block incense burner, page 82; Bowwow (020 7792 8532) for the wooden plinth, page 82; Kate Schuricht Ceramics (020 7813 7812) for the small raku vessels with glass liners, pages 120–1.

The publisher would also like to thank Helen Woodhall, Catriona Woodburn, Libby Willis, Kathie Gill and Barbara Haynes.